INSPIRING FOOTBALL STORIES

FOR KIDS

BEN BYDE

TABLE OF CONTENTS

INTRODUCTION 5

THE ICE BOWL:
"NFL'S COLDEST MATCH" 6

KURT WARNER
"THE GREATEST SHOW ON TURF" 12

THE LAST HELMETLESS PLAYER 22

TOM "THE BOMB" DEMPSEY.................................. 26

THE DOLPHINS UNBEATEN SEASON....................... 32

THE IMMACULATE RECEPTION 36

TOM BRADY... 40

THE HELMET CATCH.. 48

THE MANNING FAMILY 52

JERRY "FLASH 80" RICE....................................... 60

"THE CATCH" 68

THE BIRTH OF THE ICONIC HUDDLE...................... 74

THE "HAIL MARY" MIRACLE................................. 76

THE FIRST FOOTBALL GAME EVER........................ 78

CONCLUSION.. 81

TABLE OF CONTENTS

INTRODUCTION

Welcome to the electrifying world of football, where passion ignites the field, and dreams take flight like soaring touchdowns! Prepare to embark on an exhilarating journey through the lives of some of the most remarkable figures in the history of this incredible sport.

In this book, we'll explore the incredible stories of football legends who overcame challenges, defied the odds, and etched their names in the annals of football history. These athletes' journeys are testaments to the indomitable spirit of determination, grit, and the unwavering belief in oneself. But that's not all - we'll also venture into the captivating world of football, where the game goes beyond mere scoreboards and touchdowns.

From the bone-chilling "Ice Bowl" where the NFL's coldest match took place, to the courage of the last helmetless player, and the awe-inspiring feats of Tom "The Bomb" Dempsey and the legendary Tom Brady. We'll also delve into the enduring legacy of the Manning family and the birth of the iconic huddle that revolutionized the game.

Our journey doesn't stop there. We'll step back in time to witness the very first football game ever played, a historic moment that laid the foundation for the sport we love today.

Each of these stories is meticulously woven with fun facts, sprinkled with captivating details, which are designed to engage, entertain, and above all, inspire you. You may find yourself laughing, perhaps shedding a tear or two, but one thing is certain - you'll learn. You'll learn about resilience, the relentless pursuit of excellence, overcoming adversity, and the strength to stand tall in the face of challenges.

Winning in football isn't just about scoring touchdowns, it's about the journey, the struggles, and the triumph of the human spirit on and off the field.

So, gear up, young readers, and get ready for an electrifying ride through the highs and lows, the triumphs and trials, of football's greatest heroes and wackiest games ever played.

Remember, every legend was once a child who dared to dream.

Now, it's your turn.

The clock was ticking down and the Packers were trailing the Cowboys by three points. They were so close to the end zone but if they called a run play and it didn't work the clock would run out and they would lose. If they passed and it didn't come off then the clock would stop and they'd still have a chance at a field goal to tie the game up and send it into overtime.

It would have been a tough call in normal conditions. But given that this Wisconsin field was completely frozen, players were sliding about like it was an ice rink and the temperature with windchill was literally Arctic, a run play seemed unthinkable.

Legendary Green Bay quarterback, Bart Starr held a quick conference with his linemen, and they agreed that they thought a quarterback sneak was on. Trying to rub some life into his frostbitten fingers, Starr jogged over to run the play by his coach, the great Vince Lombardi. His reply was brief and to the point. "Then do it," he said yelling above the howling icy wind, "and let's get the hell out of here."

How do you picture a typical day at a football game? Perhaps you see an emerald green field under a clear blue sky on a chilly autumn day. You may even think of watching a fun snow game where the players celebrate touchdowns by making snow angels in the end zone. Sometimes though, the elements are so harsh that a football game can be more like a mid-winter battle of Viking armies than a sports match.

One particular game in the early days of the Super Bowl era is especially remembered for the brutal conditions endured by the fans, officials, coaching teams and players. This was the chilling and thrilling story of the legendary "Ice Bowl" between the Green Bay Packers and the Dallas Cowboys, which took place at Lambeau Field in Green Bay, Wisconsin, on December 31, 1967.

The story begins with a brutal cold snap that gripped the Midwest. The temperature was a bone-chilling minus 15 degrees Fahrenheit (-26 degrees Celsius) and the field was frozen solid, earning it the nickname The Frozen Tundra. To make things worse, a wicked wind howled, making it feel twenty degrees colder still. The conditions were insane for everyone present.

This wasn't just any regular-season game either. This was back in the days when the NFC was called the NFL and the AFC was called the AFL. They ran as two quite separate leagues but this was the second season that the winners of each league would meet in the Super Bowl. The Green Bay Packers had won the first Super Bowl the year before and they were desperate for the opportunity to defend their title. Now they were just one game away from getting that chance.

The "Ice Bowl" was the NFL Championship Game, with a ticket to Super Bowl II up for grabs. The Green Bay Packers, led by legendary coach Vince Lombardi, faced the Dallas Cowboys, a talented team led by their charismatic coach, Tom Landry, and determined to make history. It was a rematch of the previous season's NFL Championship game, which the Packers had won in Dallas, and both teams were ready for another epic battle.

The winner would be the hot favorite to win the Super Bowl against the AFL champion, but before that a very cold test lay ahead of the players on both sides, and it would prove to be one of the most demanding trials of their lives.

The players took to the field, steam rising from their breath as they prepared to do battle. The referee blew the whistle for the kick off, but when his lips froze to his whistle and his skin ripped as he took it away, the officials decided to resort to calling the game with their voices only to avoid more bleeding lips.

The frozen turf was treacherous, causing players to slip and slide as they fought for every inch. As the game began, Dallas seized the momentum. The Cowboys star quarterback, Don Meredith, connected with receiver Lance Rentzel for a 50-yard touchdown pass and the frozen home fans were silenced.

Green Bay, determined not to let the cold affect their spirit, answered back. Quarterback Bart Starr, a true ice-cold legend, orchestrated a precise drive, capping it off with a short touchdown pass to Boyd Dowler and the game was tied 7-7 at the end of the first quarter.

In the second quarter, the slippery playing field made it difficult to mount sustained drives and defense ruled. Both teams had their moments but were unable to break the deadlock and the score remained 7-7 at halftime.

The Cowboys managed to inch ahead with a field goal in the second half, but conditions were getting even worse. The game had become a grueling ordeal, with players battling not only their opponents but the freezing conditions.

With the game hanging in the balance, the Packers dug deep in the fourth quarter. Bart Starr, despite the numbing cold, engineered a crucial drive. With just over four minutes left in the game, Starr handed the ball to running back Chuck Mercein, who plunged into the end zone. The Packers had regained the lead and were 14-10.

The Cowboys, not willing to accept defeat, made one final push. Don Meredith led them down the field in the dying moments of the game. With less than a minute left, Meredith himself sneaked into the end zone, and the Cowboys went ahead 17-14.

The frozen crowd was on the edge of their seats, with the Packers trailing by three points. But then, something magical happened. Bart Starr, executed a legendary drive and with only 16 seconds left they found themselves within striking distance of the end zone.

Now the decision was whether to take the easy kick to take the game into overtime, or chance everything on a play for a touchdown. When the Packers offensive lineman agreed that there was just about enough grip on this icy frozen tundra to go for the push over, Starr and Lombardi called the daring play.

Would the gamble pay off? Or would the Packers leave the field without the fire of a victory to thaw their beaten and frostbitten bodies.

Bart Starr took the snap and he and his linemen instantly sprung forward. They were met by a wall of Cowboys defenders, but kept pushing forward. The crowd was going wild, and the players on the field were giving it their all. It was a moment that would be remembered forever.

Starr kept pushing and pushing, and finally, he broke through the mass of bodies in front of him. He lunged forward, stretching his arm out as far as he could. The ball crossed the goal line, and the referee signaled a touchdown. The Lambeau Field crowd erupted in cheers. The Packers had won the game!

It was a moment that would go down in history, and Bart Starr would forever be remembered as the hero of the Ice Bowl game. His determination and grit had led the Packers to victory, and he had done it in the final seconds of the game.

The Green Bay Packers emerged victorious with a final score of 21-17 but the Ice Bowl had been more than just a football game. It was a battle against the elements, a test of resilience, and a testament to the indomitable spirit of players and fans alike. The Packers held on to secure their spot in the Super Bowl and it was a game that players, coaches, and fans would never forget.

Everyone was utterly spent, and players were in tears in the locker room at the end of the game. Several had frostbite, including the victorious quarterback Bart Starr, and many others had flu-like symptoms. The losing quarterback Don Meredith had nothing but praise for his teammates, but it was reported that not a word was spoken by the Cowboys players on their flight home. Both sets of players had given absolutely everything.

Championship dreams had been set aside at moments when this game had seemed more like a test of survival. It was an incredible moment in NFL history, and a story that shows the unbelievable spirit and heart of the game, no matter how challenging the journey may be.

When he was asked about the decision to go for the quarterback sneak to win on the final play rather than hedge their bets and possibly settle for a game tying field goal, Vince Lombardi admitted the call was risky. "I didn't figure the people in the stands wanted to sit around in the cold any longer," he said. "I do have some compassion though I've been accused of having none!"

For decades afterwards, those who were present, whether they were on the winning side or the losing side, would be haunted by the memory of that game. They would lie in bed in their warm homes and still feel that devilish winter wind biting at their toes and gnawing at their fingers. It was a test of human endurance and strength of will that is rarely, if ever, seen in the world of sport, and a game that is etched into football folklore as one of the most iconic and dramatic moments in NFL history.

Super Bowl XXXIV was unfolding under the bright lights of the Georgia Dome, a colossal showdown between the Rams and the Titans. Amidst the giants on the field, one man stood out – Kurt Warner, the quarterback of the St. Louis Rams.

His path to this grand stage was nothing short of miraculous. A journey from obscurity, working in a grocery store, to leading the Rams in the most important game of their history as they sought to secure their first ever Super Bowl victory.

The score was deadlocked at 16-16 in the fourth quarter, the Tennessee Titans having rallied back, matching the Rams point for point in a dramatic comeback.

Warner, clad in his blue and gold uniform, could feel the immense pressure of the moment bearing down on his shoulders. With the football in his hands feeling heavier than usual,

his eyes scanned the field, darting between the oncoming defenders and his receivers looking to find his target.

Warner took a deep, grounding breath, steadying his nerves as he retreated into the pocket, ready for the pivotal throw. Time seemed to slow. He launched the ball with laser precision that had been honed through years of quiet determination. The football soared, a perfect spiral cutting through the tense air, heading towards receiver Isaac Bruce. And as the ball descended, the fate of the game, and Warner's legacy, hung delicately in the balance...

The biggest stories can sometimes grow out of the smallest places. The greatest heroes can sometimes come from the humblest beginnings. And Burlington, Iowa was certainly a humble place to come from.

This small, picturesque town was the kind of place where everyone knows each other. And in this small town on June 22nd, 1971, a baby boy named Kurtis Eugene Warner was born to a couple named Gene and Sue Warner. Kurt's parents divorced when was six, but he was always surrounded by a loving family... and lots of football fans.

Some of his happiest days were spent in the backyard with his dad and brothers, perfecting his throws and honing his skills. Football wasn't exactly Kurt's first love. He was very active as a child and played all sorts of sports and games, but he wasn't concerned with becoming a professional athlete at that stage. Kurt simply wanted to have fun.

Sure, he was good at football, but what really mattered was that he loved to play. It was like magic, and it made him feel alive.

Somewhere along the way, football became a passion, and a dream was born. He knew it would take a lot of hard work and self-belief, but Kurt was determined to one day become a professional athlete in the NFL. He had no idea just how long it would take and just how hard it would be to prove himself though.

He played quarterback for his high school's team in Cedar Rapids with great success, but he didn't attract the attention of college football programs at the very highest level. Those scouts apparently thought he was too small and too slow to make it in the big leagues. But he did secure a place at the University of Northern Iowa (UNI). UNI was a small school with big dreams, just like Kurt himself. It may not have been the perfect college for someone aiming for the highest level, but it was an opportunity, and he was ready to make his mark.

Something else happened at college though, that would prove to be even more foundational to his life than anything that happened on the football field. And bizarrely, it happened in a Country Western Bar.

It was a line dancing night, the music was soothing, and a former Marine named Brenda was there to dance and forget her worries for a few hours. She was certainly not there looking for love. She had recently divorced her first husband and left the military to care for her children, one of whom had severe disabilities. This night was just meant to give her some time to herself. But then she met this goofy college guy named Kurt and the pair hit it off.

The following day Kurt dropped in at her house having been told her address by a mutual friend and he met her son, Zach, for the first time. In her experience people always reacted unpredictably when first encountering Zach and his special needs. But Kurt just accepted him for who he was and before long the two of them were roughhousing on the floor. That was when Brenda knew that this man was worthy of being in their lives.

Kurt's relationship with Brenda would prove to be the bedrock upon which every aspect of his life would be built on. Through all the journeys Kurt was about to make following his football dreams, Brenda would be there cheering him on, sharing in his triumphs and providing the anchor in the storm that would prevent him from being washed away when all his hopes seemed to be dashed on the rocks.

For most of his college career, Kurt was a backup quarterback, but in his senior year he got the chance to lead the UNI Panthers. He was the starting quarterback in 12 games, finishing the 1993 season with an 8-4 record, and being named Offensive Player of the Year for the Gateway Conference in which the Panthers played.

Kurt had made the most of the chance that college afforded him, but would it be enough to keep his NFL dreams alive? Unfortunately, he once more found it hard to attract the recognition he deserved. This time he was overlooked by the NFL scouts and went undrafted in the 1994 NFL Draft. He had a glimmer of hope when he got the chance to try out for the Green Bay Packers' training camp later that year, but he was released before the regular season started.

It appeared that his NFL dreams were slipping away.

He still had to find a way to make a living, so he started coaching at the University of Northern Iowa. That didn't pay that well, so he also had to take a job at a grocery store working on minimum wage, stacking shelves and bagging groceries to make ends meet. He and Brenda had each other and the boys, but they must have wondered whether their lives were really heading anywhere. Yet still Kurt spent his evenings working on his football skills, never letting go of the passion that drove him.

In 1995, when it seemed like his NFL dream was dead and buried, the Arena Football League (AFL) came calling. The Iowa Barnstormers called out to Kurt and offered him a chance to prove himself. Arena football was played indoors on smaller pitches and with fewer players but here was an opportunity to play professional football, and Kurt wasn't about to waste it.

He quickly became the star quarterback for the Barnstormers and was named the Most Valuable Player (MVP) of the Arena Football League in 1996 and 1997. He led his team to the Arena Bowl (the AFL equivalent of the Super Bowl) in both seasons and the crowds adored him. It wasn't the NFL, but Kurt made the most of this time.

Life was still throwing all sorts of challenges in Kurt's way, not least when Brenda's parents died after their home was destroyed by a tornado in 1996. But this was also a time of simple blessings. Kurt's AFL career was taking off and in 1997 he and Brenda were married in the same church where Brenda's parents had been commemorated the year before.

Soon after, Kurt formally adopted Brenda's two children from her first marriage, and he fully committed to his burgeoning Christian faith making it the bedrock of his life. It was certainly a year for maturing and for the galvanizing of his spirit.

Nothing had come easy. Up until now, Kurt's life had been characterized by tough trials, precious blessings and slim opportunities. His hard work and determination had opened enough doors so that his sporting dreams still lived and breathed. But they were like glowing embers that would soon have to either burst into flame or fade out of existence. It felt as though the next break had to come soon, but the strength of Kurt's resolve was such that he was determined to grab it by the horns as soon as it came.

And that horned opportunity came in the shape of a St Louis Rams helmet!

He was never really meant to be a starter for the team, and Kurt's journey with the Rams began in a pretty unexpected way. He signed a future contract with the team after the 1997 season had ended and, as part of that contract, he went to the Netherlands in February 1998 to play for the Amsterdam Admirals in NFL Europe. He had a stellar season there, leading the league in touchdown passes and passing yards, and playing in front of the largest crowds in Admirals' history.

His performances in Europe were enough to earn him a place as a backup quarterback for the Rams' 1998 NFL season, although he was the third-string quarterback and only threw four completions from eleven attempted passes in competitive games all year. In preparation for the 1999 season, Kurt managed to work his way up to being the second-string quarterback but fellow Iowa-native, Trent Green, was all set to lead the Rams to glory. Then, fate intervened.

The start of the 1999 season was just around the corner and Dick Vermeil, head coach of the St Louis Rams, found himself in need of a starting quarterback. Trent Green had just picked up a long term injury and so he called his backup into his office to tell him that it was time for him to step up and lead the team.

Vermeil had his reservations. This guy hadn't exactly taken the typical route into the NFL after not being drafted out of college, and if there was more time he might look to a quick trade to solve the problem. Yet there was charisma about him that inspired trust and belief and sometimes that mattered more than statistics and credentials.

This man had got here the hard way and the grit and self-belief that required seemed to ooze out of him.

Vermeil regarded Kurt Warner for a while, choosing his words very carefully. "There's something special about you son," he said. "And I can't wait to find out what it is."

By handing Warner the responsibility of leading the St Louis Rams offense, Dick Vermeil had just set into motion the final stage in one of the most incredible stories in NFL history.

Kurt Warner was now the Rams' starting quarterback. He had finally reached the highest level, but for Kurt this was just the start of what he was determined to make into a career in the NFL.

He threw three touchdown passes in each of his first three games as starting quarterback – something that no one else had ever done, and a record that stood until Patrick Mahomes matched it in 2018. The Rams fourth game of the 1999 season was against the San Francisco 49ers who had beaten the Rams in each of their previous seventeen meetings. It was ridiculous to think that they might even have a chance, and yet Warner led St Louis to a 42-20 victory throwing five touchdown passes.

They had started the season 4-0 and Kurt's stellar rise from packing grocery bags had begun. The surprised response of sports fans across the country was depicted perfectly by the Sports Illustrated October magazine cover, which pictured Kurt alongside the caption, 'Who Is This Guy?"

Kurt Warner's first season as the Rams' starting quarterback turned into a magical journey, and he played a vital role in a St Louis offense that would be branded, 'The Greatest Show on Turf.' At the end of the regular season, the Rams finished 13-3, securing their first playoff berth and first division title since the team had moved to St Louis. Kurt Warner was named the league's Most Valuable Player for the season, and he remains the only undrafted player to have ever been awarded that honor.

Kurt had waited so long and worked so hard for this opportunity. He was a man who had grown accustomed to squeezing every chance that came his way to get everything he possibly could from it, and he was not about to let this miraculous season end yet.

After beating Minnesota in the Divisional round and Tampa Bay in the NFC Championship game, St Louis was heading to the Georgia Dome in Atlanta looking for its first Super Bowl title.

The Rams would face another team looking for its first title – the Tennessee Titans – and it would be one of the most thrilling Super Bowls of all time.

The first half was a largely defensive tussle, with St Louis kicking three field goals for a 9-0 lead at halftime. Kurt Warner's first touchdown pass of the game established a 16-0 lead for the Rams, but the Titans fought back hard to tie the game up in the fourth quarter before a spectacular 73-yard passing play saw Isaac Bruce score the go-ahead touchdown for the Rams.

The Titans still weren't done though. With Tennessee only one yard away from tying the game, it all came down to one final play. In the end it was ironic that after a season characterized by scintillating offense it would be the Rams' defense that ultimately won them the Super Bowl.

With just seconds left on the clock, the Titans were on the brink of a touchdown and extra point that would send the game into the first overtime in Super Bowl history. The Titans' quarterback, Steve McNair, dropped back and hurled a lightning-fast pass to wide-open receiver Kevin Dyson just five yards from the goal line. The crowd held its breath as Dyson caught that ball and made a dash for the end zone.

But then linebacker Mike Jones changed direction, zoomed across and launched himself at Dyson, wrapping his legs up in a tackle. Dyson stretched his body, reaching out with all his might but it was an inch too far. The final seconds ticked away, the Rams won the game 23-16, and the crowd went wild!

Kurt Warner had played like a superhero. He threw for a record-breaking 414 yards and 2 touchdowns. He also set the Super Bowl record for most pass attempts without an interception. The Rams won the Super Bowl, and Kurt Warner was named the Super Bowl MVP, becoming only the sixth player to be named NFL MVP and Super Bowl MVP in the same season – a feat that no one else had achieved at the time or would achieve until Patrick Mahomes in the 2022 season.

To the world, it seemed as though Warner had come out of nowhere to achieve the highest possible honors and it was an incredible story. But this is not a story of good fortune.

Kurt had worked and worked and worked to get to where he was. He had seized every unlikely opportunity he had been given and used each one to clamber his way up to the next step until finally he reached the top.

He would enjoy an incredible three years in St Louis, leading one of the finest offenses the NFL had ever seen and even managed to take the Rams back to one more Super Bowl. But the next few seasons after that would see no repeat of their spectacular displays in the 'Greatest Show on Turf' era.

In 2004, Kurt Warner was released by the St Louis Rams and, after a stint with the New York Giants, signed for the Arizona Cardinals in 2005. At this point, many thought his best days were behind him. He had a few tough seasons where he had to battle for his starting place but in 2008, things began to turn around.

He led the Cardinals to the NFC West Division title and their first playoff berth in ten years, including a fabulous December win over his old team, the St Louis Rams. He then led the team to playoff victories over the Atlanta Falcons at home and the Panthers in Carolina, before throwing four touchdown passes in the NFC championship game against Philadelphia to book the Cardinals' first ever appearance in the Super Bowl. It was also a season that saw him named as the NFC Pro Bowl starting quarterback. It was a magical journey for the team and their quarterback, and they came so close to winning it all, before eventually going down 27-23 to the Pittsburgh Steelers. Despite the loss, he became only the sixth quarterback in history to throw touchdown passes in three different Super Bowls and had the impressive record of having guided his teams to Super Bowl appearances in each and every one of the three seasons in which he started every game.

The 2009 season would be Kurt Warner's last in the NFL. It was a great way to finish, only missing one game due to a concussion and leading his team into the playoffs once more. After an incredible 51-45 win over Green Bay in the highest scoring NFL playoff game ever in the wildcard round, the Cardinals lost to the New Orleans Saints in a game that saw Warner leave the game after a big hit.

In a stunning career revival, Kurt Warner led the Arizona Cardinals to their first Super Bowl in 2008, dazzling fans by outshining his past glories. He masterfully steered the team to victories against formidable opponents, culminating in a historic yet heartbreakingly close Super Bowl loss.

Warner's final seasons, marked by record-breaking performances and an epic playoff win, solidified his legacy as a legendary quarterback who defied expectations until his retirement.

He formally announced his retirement in January 2010 saying that he was looking forward to spending more time with wife and being a true father to his seven children.

Kurt Warner delivered countless thrilling moments on the field. From epic touchdown passes to breath-taking comeback victories, he left a mark on the game that will be remembered for years to come.

He was, of course, inducted into the Pro Football Hall of Fame – a place where the legends of the game are forever celebrated. But what really makes Kurt Warner's story incredible is the journey he had to take to get to the very top of his sport.

Kurt Warner's entire career was a come-from-behind victory, and it is a testament to perseverance, hard work, and never giving up on your dreams. His journey from humble beginnings as a grocery store clerk to NFL stardom is a reminder that with determination, belief in yourself, and a lot of hard work, you can achieve the impossible. He credited his stellar rise and outstanding career to the supportive influences of his family, his teammates, and God.

So, if you have a dream, whether it's sporting or not, remember the incredible tale of Kurt Warner. Never give up, even when faced with adversity, and be ready to make the most of every opportunity that comes your way even if it wasn't the particular opportunity you were hoping for. Kurt Warner's story is a lesson that dreams do come true with hard work, self-belief, and perhaps just a touch of destiny.

THE LAST HELMETLESS PLAYER

On November 6, 1938, the Chicago Bears were playing a home game against the Green Bay Packers. Back then the Bears played their home games at Wrigley field, where a football field was squeezed into the baseball stadium so tightly that the end zone finished quite abruptly in a brick wall that marked the edge of the outfield. It made for a brilliantly electric atmosphere where the fans were right on top of the action. The Chicago fans were roaring their team on as they rampaged into the red zone in the first quarter.

The ball was snapped back to Chicago quarterback, Ray Buivid, and he instinctively scanned the field, checking down his mental list of passing options. Then he saw him. Dick Plasman had got some separation from his man and was heading into the end zone begging for the ball. Buivid launched it; Plasman stretched up to the sky, his eyes focused solely on the football. And without ever breaking stride... he crashed straight into that brick wall at the end of the field.

Players and fans alike fell silent in shock as Plasman collapsed in a crumbled blood heap. The sickening crunch would have drawn horrified gasps in any era of football. But this particular collision was genuinely life-threatening... because Dick Plasman was not wearing a helmet.

In the early days of football, players charged out onto the field with their faces set in grim determination and their heads completely unprotected. It was a savage time, and the warriors of the NFL faced a brutal battlefield without the armor we take for granted today. It was common for players to grow their hair relatively long to offer them some protection, but this of course didn't do much when there was a full head-on collision.

In those early days, football was like a wild west showdown. Helmets weren't even a glimmer in anyone's eye. Players faced bone-crushing tackles, ducked flying elbows, and dodged rogue knees with nothing but grit and maybe a handlebar mustache for luck.

By the time the NFL formed in 1920, some manner of protective headgear was worn by the majority of players. These early helmets had already evolved from little more than a head harness and caps made from moleskin, to padded leather headpieces with flaps and ear holes. Along the way other features such as nose guards were experimented with before being discarded because they hindered vision, breathing and rarely stayed in place.

These early helmets were still more like flimsy hats with some extra padding though. They were not much more protective than a well-worn baseball cap. Yet, the leatherhead was a step in the right direction, a sign that maybe, just maybe, brains were worth protecting.

In time more innovations came along, and it wasn't long before leather helmets were designed to 'cradle' the skull and absorb and distribute any impact in such a way that serious head injuries were greatly reduced (though they probably still left the field with a headache or two).

By the 1930s, a bar across the face of a helmet became a fairly standard feature, but this had also taken about twenty years to evolve from a crude rubber-covered wire into something that offered some genuine protection.

Team logos did not begin to appear in any standard form until the late 1940s, but it was still common practice to paint protective headgear purely so that quarterbacks were able to distinguish between receivers and defenders downfield.

In this era when men were made of steel, and football was a dance with danger, Dick Plasman was a force to be reckoned with and his determination was unmatched. But what set Plasman apart wasn't just his skill; it was the fact that he charged onto the battlefield without any sort of helmet at all, a lone wolf in a sea of protective headgear.

Picture him, eyes ablaze, tearing through the defensive line like a hurricane. Opponents, clad in their protective helmets, couldn't help but be awestruck by the man who dared to face the storm bare-headed. It was unconventional, daring, and just a little bit crazy.

By the time Dick Plasman became a pro, helmets had become standard and prevented a huge number of long-term serious injuries for football players. But they were not mandatory, and Plasman took pride in being tough enough to not wear one.

Plasman had been drafted by the Bears in 1937 as a man who could do a lot of different things on the football field. He was a pass-catching tight end, linebacker and kicker, and did it all with a ferocious temper that earned him the nickname 'Eric the Red.' The Chicago Bears did not mind this sort of attitude at all though. This was a team that reveled in their own reputation as the 'Monsters of the Midway.'

But after that horrific collision between Plasman and the brick wall at Wrigley Field, many of his monster teammates had to look away in fright.

"He hit it head on, full stride, and peeled his whole scalp off his head," teammate Dick Schweidler reported. Several were convinced he was dead, unable to see how anyone could live through that impact.

Dick Plasman lost consciousness instantly and had to be stretched back to the locker room. There was blood everywhere and at least an arm was clearly broken.

But he did soon regain consciousness once he was off the field and receiving medical attention. And the first thing he said was, "Did we win?"

His mother was apparently convinced that he would never play again, but he did. In fact, he helped the Bears to back-to-back NFL championships in 1940 and 1941. But things were about to change, and Dick Plasman would be remembered as the NFL's last helmetless player.

Protective headgear became mandatory in college football in 1939 and plastic helmets first appeared in the 1940s. The world was deep in World War II. The NFL, like the rest of the country, was feeling the pinch. Leather was scarce and rubber was rationed. But plastic was a new possibility. Plastic helmets were lighter and more durable than their leather counterparts, but they were about as stylish as a bowl of oatmeal. Still, the NFL was evolving, and so were its helmets.

In 1943, the winds of change sweeping through the league became law. The NFL, perhaps recognizing the value of protecting its stars, officially mandated the use of helmets for all players. Dick Plasman, the last of the helmetless wonders, reluctantly joined the ranks of protected heads. It was the end of an era, the last gasp of helmetless glory.

No longer could a player channel the spirit of Dick Plasman and charge into the fray with the wind in their hair. Helmets were here to stay, a symbol of progress and safety in a sport that was rapidly becoming more than just a game.

In the years that followed, Dick Plasman's helmetless escapades became the stuff of legend. Old-timers would gather around the fire, regaling youngsters with tales of the man who defied convention, charging into battle with nothing but his wits and a thick head of hair.

The rough and tumble history of NFL helmets has come a long way and players' protective technology continues to evolve.

The legacy of Dick Plasman endures, not just as a footnote in NFL history but as a symbol of a time when the game was wild and untamed.

So, as you watch the modern warriors of the gridiron, donned in their high-tech helmets, take a moment to appreciate the helmets that safeguard their health.

And remember also, the rebel who played without a helmet, blazing through the history books of football lore.

Sometimes, it takes a little madness to leave a permanent mark and memory on the game we love.

TOM "THE BOMB" DEMPSEY

It was November 8th, 1970, and a football game was in progress at Tulane Stadium in New Orleans. The clock was almost at zero and the Saints were a point down to the visiting Detroit Lions. It had not been a great season so far and the glimmer of hope that the New Orleans faithful had held earlier in the game, that this might be a precious victory for their beloved team, was now all but extinguished. They may have only been a point behind but there were only seconds left and the Saints were still in their own half.

The Lions could taste victory and when they realized that the opposition were setting up for a field goal, they weren't too worried. This was back in the days when the goal posts were on the goal line at the front of the end zone rather than the end line at the back of the end zone, but this was still going to be a field goal attempt of over 60 yards. When the Lions saw the New Orleans's kicker jogging out onto the field there were even a few sniggers.

Tom Dempsey had been born with half a right foot that had no toes... and this was the foot he kicked with.

The New Orleans's kicking team got into their pre-snap huddle and Dempsey's words were simple: "Fellas, this is going to be a pretty long one, so give me an extra second of blocking." Eyebrows were raised amongst his teammates. 'Pretty long one' was quite the understatement. If he made this, it would be a record-breaking one...

Tom Dempsey was born in Milwaukee on January 12, 1947 with a birth defect that meant he had no toes on his right foot and no fingers on his right hand. Tom's family weren't wealthy but his dad, Carl, worked hard to put food on the table, and his mom, Shirley, was the queen of encouragement. The family moved to California when Tom was young, and it was here that he spent most of his childhood.

Growing up, Tom faced the usual trials of childhood as well as a few that were unique to him. The neighborhood kids teased him about his crooked foot and sometimes that really got to him. He would have moments of self-doubt, questioning his ability to do even everyday things. Due to the limitations of his right hand and right foot, it was harder for him to learn to do many things that the other kids took for granted, such as tie his shoes or use a knife and fork. Yet through the support of those around him he was able to use these trials as a motivation, and what many would label his physical weaknesses became the source of his mental strength.

"There's no such word as can't," his father would tell him as he made him try everything and keep trying until he succeeded. It wasn't long before Tom was his own motivator and he adopted the mentality that everything was possible for him, even if it just took him a little longer than it did for his peers. And soon it wasn't enough for him to simply be able to do something – he would not be satisfied until he was good at everything he tried.

He played football at High School, but at that stage no one thought of him ever being able to kick the ball. He was a defensive lineman back then and would play in a right boot that had been sawn in half and sewn up. Tom would have moments of feeling sorry for himself, but he was lucky enough to have a coach who saw him exactly the same as every other player on the team. He would encourage him to keep on working, just like his dad had.

His foot still attracted snide comments from his opposition, but on the football field he was able to deal with those naysayers in ways that would have always gotten him in trouble if he had reacted to the kids in the neighborhood in the same way.

"Aw, this guy can't do anything," his opposing lineman would say. Then the ball would snap, and Tom would thunder into them making it quite clear that there was plenty he could do.

As the final whistle blew on his high school football days, Tom's head was buzzing with dreams of making it big. College was calling, and he answered, strapping on his helmet for the Palomar College Comets. It was a step up, and Tom was ready to take the leap.

Now, college football is a beast of its own, with fierce competition and big guys eyeing the same dream. Life was hard, both in the classroom and on the football field. Tom had his fair share of fumbles and he began to wonder whether this might be as far as his playing career would take him. But Tom was made of grit and determination.

About halfway through his college career Tom began kicking footballs. It must have been crazy to see as he first tried it, but it soon became apparent that this kid had a talent for sending the ball through the sticks.

He still wore a sawn-off shoe on his kicking foot, but he used tape across the front of the foot stub. It was harder for him to kick the ball straight than for kickers with more typically shaped kicking feet, but he could kick it a long way.

He was a former lineman after all, and he was able to put a lot of power into those kicks.

But the journey from college to the NFL isn't a leisurely stroll. Tom had to prove himself, and the scouts weren't handing out golden tickets. The NFL Draft is the moment every aspiring footballer holds their breath for. But Tom's name wasn't called on draft day.

Was he disappointed? Sure. But did he throw in the towel? Not a chance.

In 1970, Tom found himself wearing a New Orleans Saints jersey and wearing a specially made $200 (that would be over $1,500 in today's money) boot instead of the sawn-off and taped up versions that had seen him through college. New Orleans was a team that wasn't exactly ruling the football kingdom, but they took a chance on Tom. They saw something special in that guy with the crooked foot and signed him up.

In the season leading up to the game against Detroit, Dempsey's record had been mediocre at best, having only made five of fifteen field goal attempts. The Saints had only managed one win and their Head Coach Tom Fears had just been replaced.

Perhaps it was the hope brought on by having a new head coach, JD Roberts, or just the sense that things couldn't get any worse, but there was a buzz around the stadium ahead of the game against the Lions. There was a sense that something special might be in the air.

Almost 67,000 fans crammed into Tulane stadium and Tom Dempsey, with his mismatched cleats and a grin that could light up Louisiana, was ready for action.

The game kicked off and the Lions and the Saints began battling like gladiators in the Roman Colosseum. Both teams were tentative in the first quarter, like boxers in the early rounds of a championship fight, and the only score was a Tom Dempsey field goal from 29 yards. The Lions struck back with a touchdown in the second quarter to take the lead and the only response the Saints could muster before half time was another Tom Dempsey field goal from 27 yards.

The Lions scored first in the second half as quarterback Bill Munson threw a 2-yard touchdown pass to Charlie Sanders to extend the Detroit lead to 14-6. There was a fresh determination to the Saints under their new coach though, and every man wanted to prove their worth to their new boss.

The Saints offense drove to within a few yards of the end zone but in the end, had to settle for another three points from the boot of Tom Dempsey. Tom was doing his job perfectly, and was keeping his team in contention, but he'd rather be kicking touchdown conversions than field goals.

He finally got his chance to do that in the fourth quarter after Tom Barrington scored a 4-yard rushing touchdown to put the Saints ahead. Tom Dempsey added the extra point, and the New Orleans faithful were beginning to believe.

That belief was knocked out of them a few minutes later though when a late Detroit drive ended in an 18-yard Errol Mann field goal to put the Lions up 17-16 with only seconds left. After a kickoff return and a quick passing play to move the ball up the field as far as they could, the Saints' kicking team took to the field in hope rather than expectation.

Most people thought the game was over. Even most of the New Orleans's players thought that this field goal attempt was pushing the limits of what was humanly possible. But they knew they had to give it a try. They had a one-of-a-kind kicker with an incredible right foot, in more ways than one! They had to give Dempsey a shot, because you never know.

Several of the Lions players could actually be heard giggling as they lined up for the final play of the game. They had already seen this guy kick the ball through the sticks four times that day, but all those attempts had been from under 30 yards. This would be from more than sixty.

Perhaps Tom heard the sniggers of his opposition. If he did, it only served to fuel his determination for the record-breaking attempt he was about to make.

The referee blew his whistle. The long snapper, Jackie Burkett, slung the ball back right on target. The catch and presentation of the ball from the holder, Joe Scarpati, was perfect. And then Tom Dempsey swung his half a right boot through the air and sent the ball on its way with a thunderous impact.

It was clear straight away that it had a chance. With every end-over-end rotation of the ball through the crisp Louisiana air, the desperate Saints fans leaned a little further forward, and their eyes grew a little wider.

And with every yard the ball traveled the sniggers of the Lions players grew a little quieter.

The ball split the uprights and dropped over the crossbar with only inches to spare. The stadium erupted, and history was made. Television commentator Jerry Romig had to repeat it several times as if to convince himself of what he was seeing: "It's good! It's good! It's good! Saints win! Saints win!"

Dempsey's teammates flooded the pitch and swarmed over him as the elation of a once-in-a-lifetime moment completely eclipsed all the heartache of their season so far. For the moment at least, they were part of something truly miraculous.

Tom Dempsey's 63-yard field goal not only sealed the victory for the Saints but also shattered records like a sledgehammer through glass. It was seven yards longer than the previous longest successful field goal and it would be more than forty years until it was surpassed. Matt Prater finally hit a 64-yard field goal in 2013, but that wasn't a last second game-winner like Dempsey's. Justin Tucker eventually made a 66-yard final play game-winning field goal in 2021. And guess who was on the losing side of that one again – the poor old Detroit Lions.

No other kicker would battle through the physical difficulties that Tom Dempsey had though. He became an instant folk hero, and his face was plastered on newspapers and TV screens across the nation.

Not everyone was thrilled. The grumpy old football purists grumbled about how Dempsey's kick was a fluke, and some even suggested that his specially made boot gave him an unfair advantage as a kicker. Years later some very clever scientists would conduct some experiments to show that, if anything, the shape of Tom's kicking foot increased the margin for error and made it harder for him to kick accurately when compared with any other.

THE DOLPHINS UNBEATEN SEASON

In December of 2005, the Miami Dolphins were hosting the New York Jets in a regular season game at Dolphins Stadium. But up in one of the suites two Dolphins legends, former coach Don Shula and retired quarterback Bob Griese, were focusing their attention on a TV screen showing a game between the Indianapolis Colts and the San Diego Chargers.

It was a tight game, but the Chargers eventually won, registering the first Colts' loss of the season, after winning their first thirteen games. Griese and Shula turned to one another and clinked their glasses together. They were still the only team in NFL history to complete a perfect season.

Legend has it that every season of the NFL, when the last remaining undefeated team in the league falls to their first defeat, players from the 1972 Dolphins team meet together in twos and threes wherever they are in the country and pop champagne to celebrate another year of their record going unmatched. This is probably something of an urban legend though. The 1972 Dolphins' running back, Mercury Morris once said that it would be nice if another team did match their feat because then they'd have other players to talk to about it.

"It's like trying to describe to someone what it's like to walk on the moon," he said. "It's only a description – they'll never know until they go."

The incredible achievement of that Dolphins team was a lot like being the first men to walk on the moon. In fact, their achievement was perhaps even greater than the lunar landing because no other team has ever reached that level since!

That perfect season began in January of 1972 in the wake of Miami's loss in Super Bowl VI to the Dallas Cowboys. Coach Don Shula vowed then that they would not only return to the Super Bowl the following year, but they would win it. At training camp later that year Shula made the whole team watch video of their Super Bowl defeat twice and the Dolphins' goal for the upcoming season was established: to go one better.

The long road to the Super Bowl began on September 2, 1972. The Dolphins were ready to hit the field for their season opener against the Cleveland Browns. The energy amongst the expectant Miami fans was electric as the teams clashed, and the Dolphins set the tone for the season with a thrilling victory. Quarterback Bob Griese and agile running back Larry Csonka showcased their skills in a spectacular display of teamwork. The crowd roared, the sun beamed down, and the Dolphins kicked off their journey with a victorious splash.

As the season progressed, the Dolphins faced formidable opponents, but they weren't fazed. The Minnesota Vikings and the Buffalo Bills pushed them closest in October, but the season continued to unfold like a magical tapestry of victories.

Griese's pinpoint passes and Csonka's powerful runs became the stuff of legends.

Mid-October saw a seed of doubt sown in the minds of Dolphins fans when Bob Griese broke his ankle. In stepped veteran backup quarterback Earl Morrall to lead the team from Week 5 onwards. His second game saw Miami face divisional rivals the Buffalo Bills in what would be the toughest test of the regular season. Buffalo led at halftime, but the Dolphins' belief was insurmountable, and they eventually came out with a one-point victory.

As the fourteen-game regular season reached an end, the Dolphins found themselves in what many had believed was an impossible position with a perfect 14-0 record. The stadium erupted in cheers, and the players reveled in the sweet taste of triumph, but only for a moment – these Dolphins weren't done making waves.

They dove into the playoffs with gusto and after defeating the Cleveland Browns, faced the Pittsburgh Steelers in the AFC Championship game. Despite having the superior record, Miami had to travel to Pittsburgh because of the rotational basis on which home field advantage was decided back then, and it was to be their toughest test yet.

The Steelers jumped up to a 7-0 lead in the first quarter before an inventive fake punt play on a fourth down put Earl Morrall in a position to deliver a 9-yard touchdown pass to Csonka and tie the game up at halftime. Morrall was not having a great game though and shortly after the Steelers retook the lead with a third quarter field goal, Don Shula replaced him with Bob Griese, now recovered from his injury.

It was as if it was written in the stars. Griese went on to orchestrate an 80-yard drive and then a 49-yard drive, both finished off by short touchdown runs from Jim Kiick to give Miami a 21-10 lead. Pittsburgh got one touchdown back, but two interceptions from the Dolphins' defense late on secured the victory and a place in Super Bowl VII.

The big game arrived, and on January 14, 1973, the Dolphins faced the mighty Washington Redskins. The sun had almost set on a remarkable season, but the Miami Dolphins had one more epic chapter to write. The stakes were sky-high as both teams eyed the coveted Vince Lombardi Trophy.

As the game kicked off, the tension in the stadium was palpable. The Dolphins, sporting their iconic aqua uniforms, took the field with determination. The first quarter unfolded with both teams testing each other's defenses.

Griese orchestrated precise plays, and the Dolphins gained a first quarter advantage with a 28-yard touchdown pass from Griese to Howard Twilley. Jim Kiick ran in a second quarter to hand the Dolphins a 14-0 halftime lead.

The Dolphins, with a lead in hand, unleashed a dazzling array of plays in the second quarter. Griese, the maestro of the gridiron, connected with star receiver Paul Warfield for a breathtaking touchdown. The Dolphins' defense, a wall of determination, held strong, denying the Redskins any chance of a comeback.

Larry Csonka, the powerhouse running back, bulldozed through the Redskins' defense, adding to the Dolphins' lead. By halftime, the score stood at 14-0 in favor of the Dolphins. The fans, wrapped in a sea of aqua and orange, could hardly contain their excitement. The perfect season was within reach.

The Dolphins' defense took over in the second half. After a scoreless third quarter the Dolphins were on the cusp of history as Griese, a picture of poise, led the offense in a clock-eating drive in the fourth. The Redskins fought back with a touchdown, but the Dolphins' lead was too substantial to overcome, and the score stood at 14-7 at the final whistle. The stadium erupted in cheers, confetti rained down, and the Dolphins made history as the first and only team to achieve a perfect season, crowned with a Super Bowl triumph.

The players hoisted the Lombardi Trophy high, and the celebration spilled over into the streets of Miami. A victory parade painted the city in aqua and orange, with fans young and old cheering for their conquering heroes.

And so the tale of the Miami Dolphins' perfect season reached its triumphant conclusion. A journey that began with a kickoff, danced through midseason drama, braved the December chill, and climaxed with a Super Bowl victory for the ages. The Dolphins, with their fins held high, etched their names in the records of football history.

So, with each new NFL season keep an eye on how long teams can sustain an undefeated run. Perhaps one day another team will rise that is great enough to share the very top step with the 1972 Dolphins. But until then, when the last undefeated team in each season finally falls to their first loss of the year, think of those retired Miami legends meeting up in small exclusive groups to clink their glasses together and remember that perfect season.

THE IMMACULATE RECEPTION

The date was December 23, and the Steelers were playing the Oakland Raiders, led by legendary coach John Madden, in the Wildcard round of the playoffs. The score was 7-6 to the Raiders and despite the low score, everyone watching this game was utterly engrossed in the contest. It was like a wrestling match between two equally matched giants or a game of chess between two grand masters. There was only one point in it, but it felt like even less than that.

But as the seconds ticked away the task facing the Steelers began to look impossible and some Raiders fans were already beginning their celebrations. Pittsburgh was on fourth down, but as there was only 22 seconds left in the game and they had no timeouts left, the down didn't really make much difference. Whatever way you looked at it, there was only time for one more play.

The biggest problem though was that the Steelers were still only on their own 40-yard line – a long, long way from the end zone and the score they needed to snatch the win.

As the Steelers broke from their huddle to roll the dice for one last time, rookie full back Franco Harris ran through his blocking assignment in his head. Then the words of his old college coach drifted into his mind, that nugget of go-to wisdom f when all else fails on the football field: "Go to the ball."

Franco had a feeling that something crazy might happen on this desperate last play. If the ball was there, he was going to go for it. What did they have to lose?

1972 was the year of the Miami Dolphins perfect regular season. But as the Dolphins were enjoying a well-earned bye week in the first round of the postseason, a truly extraordinary game was played out at the Three Rivers Stadium in Pittsburgh, Pennsylvania.

Fans were bundled up like burritos in their team colors. Christmas was just around the corner, and they were about to be presented with a truly iconic moment in sporting history, as a festive treat. The chilly air was filled with the promise of something very special.

The whistle blew, and the game kicked off like a rocket. The Raiders and the Steelers clashed like titans; each play a strategic move in this gridiron chess match. It wasn't just a game; it was a showdown between two football powerhouses.

Defenses were most definitely on top in the first half and the score was still 0-0 at halftime. Pittsburgh had come closest to scoring when they took a chance on a fourth and two on the Oakland 31-yard line, electing to go for a run and the first down rather than bagging the three-point field goal.

Unfortunately for Pittsburgh, running back John Fuqua's run was stopped in its tracks by Raiders safety Jack Tatum and they turned the ball over on downs. This would not be the last or most significant collision between these two players that day though.

The Steelers finally took the lead with a field goal in the third quarter. Raiders quarterback Daryle Lamonica then threw his second interception of the game prompting John Madden to bench him for Kenny Stabler. It didn't look as though this new Oakland quarterback was going to fare much better though as he fumbled the ball handing possession back to the Steelers, who then added another field goal for a 6-0 lead.

But then Stabler came good and led the Raiders down the field and into the end zone, which gave kicker George Blanda the chance to put Oakland into the lead. His kick was good, and the score was 7-6 with little over a minute left.

The steelers suddenly had their backs against the wall. They would need a special drive to save this game. Pittsburgh was desperate to turn the tide and pushed hard. But the clock ticked down like the suspenseful soundtrack of a blockbuster movie and they soon found themselves out of timeouts with only 22 seconds left, and still sixty yards from the end zone.

The faithful Pittsburgh fans still had hope and there was an air of anticipation about the stadium, as if everyone knew that something amazing might be about to unfold. What followed would go down in NFL history as one of the most incredible plays of all time.

"Hang onto your hats, here come the Steelers out of the huddle," announced the commentator on Steelers radio. "Twenty-two seconds remaining. It's down to one big play, fourth down and 10 yards to go. Terry Bradshaw at the controls."

Pittsburgh coach Chuck Noll called a pass to rookie receiver Barry Pearson, but when the ball was snapped the pressure from the Raiders defenders – especially linemen Tony Cline and Horace Jones – was so great that quarterback Terry Bradshaw had to scramble through his options. He dropped back to pass and then got out of the pocket to his right. The Raiders' defense, a wall of might, charged like bulls and in the chaos, Bradshaw only just got the ball away. It sailed through the frigid winter air over midfield, a frozen moment in time.

It was heading for John Fuqua, but once more Jake Tatum arrived to spoil things. He collided with the Pittsburgh full back at the same time that the football arrived, and the impact caused the ball to ricochet back several yards.

"Bradshaw, trying to get away. And his pass is…broken up by Tatum," the television commentator announced as the ball flew out of shot. But the next thing everyone knew, the ball was in the hands of Franco Harris and the rookie was streaking down the field. He passed Raiders linebacker Gerald Irons and got a block from teammate John McMakin on Phil Villapiano. One final stiff arm on defensive end Jimmy Warren and Harris was into the end zone.

"Franco Harris has it!" the television announcer continued in disbelief. "And he's over! Franco Harris grabbed the ball, a deflection! Five seconds to go! He grabbed it with five seconds to go and scored!"

The referee signaled the touchdown, and the crowd went bananas. It was a play so wild, so unpredictable, that even Hollywood scriptwriters would think it too far-fetched. But this was not fiction; this was the NFL, where fantastical stories play out on a 100-yard stage.

As the final whistle blew, the Steelers emerged victorious with a score of 13-7. The Raiders, valiant in defeat, could only shake their heads in disbelief. The 'Immaculate Reception' (as the play soon became known) would become a legendary tale, whispered in awe by football fans for generations to come.

In the post-game interviews, players struggled to put the magic of that play into words. It could be said that Franco Harris was simply in the right place at the right time. Sometimes that's all it takes to make history.

There were those on the Raiders' side of the divide however who could not believe that the play had been legal. Many insisted that the ball had bounced off of Tatum's helmet – something that would have made the pass incomplete under the rules of the time. Others were convinced that the ball had touched the ground before Franco Harris scooped it up. But these were the days before television reviews and the only opinions that really mattered in the end were those of the officials.

John Madden always said that he never got over that play and was infuriated mostly by the length of time it took for the referee to make his final signal. But make it he did, and he signaled the touchdown that ultimately swung the game in Pittsburgh's favor.

And so, the story of the 1972 NFL clash between the Oakland Raiders and the Pittsburgh Steelers entered the annals of football folklore. The Immaculate Reception became a testament to the unpredictable, heart-stopping beauty of the game.

Sometimes in the world of sports, magic happens when you least expect it. So, keep your eyes on the field, for you never know when a legendary play might unfold before your very eyes.

TOM BRADY

It was February 5, 2017, and Super Bowl LI was about halfway through the third quarter. The Atlanta Falcons had just scored another touchdown to go up by 25 points and the great Tom Brady was sitting on the sideline on his own with his head in his hands.

He had already won the Super Bowl four times and established the New England Patriots as the NFL's dominant team for several seasons, and still this really hurt. He hated losing, but this was something else. This was a total humiliation on the biggest stage. It was impossible to think that a team might come back from 28-3 down with not much more than twenty minutes left in a Super Bowl... or was it.

Tom lifted his head and allowed himself to dream, just a little. He was used to not having much of a chance. Most people would think, "We don't have a hope." But Tom Brady is not most people.

"What a comeback this would be," he mumbled to himself with the faintest of smiles. He grabbed his helmet, stood up and strode back out onto the field to do his job.

On August 3, 1977, in the picturesque town of San Mateo, California, a young boy was born. There didn't seem to be anything particularly exceptional about this boy, although his parents thought he was the most perfect thing in the world. At that stage though, not even his devoted parents could possibly have known that this bouncing baby boy would grow up to be labeled by many as the greatest quarterback in the history of the National Football League.

And this was to be a hallmark of Tom Brady's life and career as a professional football player. No one really thought he was capable of something until he had actually done it. No one that is except the people who knew him best: his coaches, his teammates, his family, and of course himself.

Tom Brady's journey began in a household filled with love for sports. His parents, Tom Sr. and Galynn, were his biggest cheerleaders from the start. As a toddler, Tom could often be found throwing a mini football across the living room and his mom soon mastered the art of ducking just in time.

As he grew older, Tom's passion for sports intensified. Baseball, basketball, and of course, football, captured his heart. He played in the neighborhood with friends until the street lights flickered on, signaling the end of another day filled with laughter and friendly competition.

Tom's family was a bit like a team in itself. He had three older sisters, Maureen, Julie, and Nancy, who were like his first set of teammates. Legend has it that Tom honed his competitive edge playing board games with his sisters, determined to win even in the fiercest battles of Monopoly. His sisters, like any good teammates, teased and encouraged him in equal measure. "You'll thank us for this someday, Tommy!" they'd laugh, as they stole his last dollar ruthlessly.

In Junipero Serra high school, Tom's skills on the football field began to shine. But it wasn't always touchdowns and victory dances for young Tom. During his junior year, he found himself riding the bench when he wanted nothing less than the number one spot. This might have crushed the spirit of a lesser athlete, but Tom used this time to study the game, learn from his coaches, and develop the resilience that would later define his career.

Before long, he emerged as his school's star quarterback. His teammates at the time were probably the first to see the inhuman competitive drive of Tom Brady when he dragged them back to his house to study plays on film while his mom prepared lunch for everybody.

After high school, Tom packed his bags and headed to the University of Michigan, where he joined the Wolverines football team. It was a dream come true, but he quickly realized that dreams require hard work and dedication.

Again, he faced fierce competition for the coveted starting quarterback position. Week after week, he pushed himself to the limit, determined to prove that he belonged on the field. And prove it, he did. By the time he graduated in 1999, Tom Brady had become a legend in maize and blue, the University of Michigan colors.

Tom entered the NFL Draft but his name was not called until the sixth round, with the 199th overall pick. Many teams had passed on him, perhaps underestimating the determination and skill that burned within this young quarterback.

As pick after pick was called, Tom's frustration grew. But then the New England Patriots took a chance on him in the sixth round. The Patriots, under the leadership of head coach Bill Belichick, were on the lookout for a quarterback who could bring a fresh spark to their team.

"You'll never regret drafting me," he assured Patriots owner Robert Kraft. As it turned out, Kraft was getting the steal of the century.

As Tom arrived at the Patriots' training camp, he faced a tough challenge. Drew Bledsoe, a Pro Bowl quarterback, was firmly entrenched as the team's starter. But this was not a new position to be in for Tom who had waited and worked for his starting chance in high school and college. He could do the same in the NFL.

Football is a game of opportunity and, as it turned out, fate had something special in store for Tom. Early in the 2001 season, destiny knocked on Tom Brady's door in the most unexpected way. During a game against the New York Jets, Drew Bledsoe suffered a devastating hit that sidelined him with an injury. This unexpected twist thrust Tom into the spotlight.

With a mixture of nerves and determination, Tom took the field as the starting quarterback for the New England Patriots. The pressure was immense, but he embraced the challenge with the same cool demeanor and drive to succeed that would become his trademark.

As the starting quarterback, Tom faced a trial by fire. The Patriots were a team with potential, but they needed a leader to guide them now that Drew Bledsoe was out. Tom seized his opportunity, showcasing a level of maturity and poise that belied his rookie status.

Apparently, Brady had assured his former high school coach that he only needed a chance to start for the Patriots and they would never go back to Drew Bledsoe. This may have been a bold statement, even for someone with the insane levels of self-belief of Tom Brady but, as it turned out, he did only need one chance to prove himself.

Week after week, he displayed a remarkable connection with his teammates, orchestrating the offense with precision. His ability to read defenses, make quick decisions, and deliver accurate passes earned the respect of players, coaches, fans and the press.

As the regular season ended, the Patriots with Tom Brady at the helm had earned a playoff berth. In the AFC Championship Game, they faced the mighty Pittsburgh Steelers, and Tom led his team to a stunning victory, securing a spot in Super Bowl XXXVI.

The Super Bowl was a showdown against the heavily favored St. Louis Rams. The Patriots, led by their unassuming quarterback, faced the daunting task of taking on the "Greatest Show on Turf" – a Rams offense that was widely touted as one of the best the league had ever seen. The game was a nail-biter, with both teams locked in a fierce battle.

With less than two minutes remaining, the score tied at 17-17, Tom Brady orchestrated a masterful drive down the field. The clock ticked away as he calmly completed pass after pass, setting up kicker Adam Vinatieri for a game-winning field goal. The kick sailed through the uprights as time expired, and the New England Patriots became Super Bowl champions.

To cap off his fairy-tale season, Tom Brady was named the Most Valuable Player (MVP) of Super Bowl XXXVI. The once-overlooked sixth-round draft pick had not only become the starting quarterback for the New England Patriots but had also led them to a Super Bowl victory in a storybook fashion.

As confetti rained down on the field, Tom hoisted the Lombardi Trophy, and the world witnessed the birth of a football legend. The journey from a draft day snub to Super Bowl MVP was complete, and Tom Brady had etched his name into the annals of NFL history. The Patriot Way, under the guidance of Brady and Belichick, had begun its reign of success.

The early 2000s would become a golden era that would redefine the standard for success in the NFL. Tom Brady - along with the brilliant mind of Coach Bill Belichick - was to spearhead a dynasty that would leave an indelible mark on the history of the sport.

Fresh off their Super Bowl victory, the Patriots set their sights on reaching the very top again. The 2002 season saw them narrowly miss the playoffs, but they roared back in 2003 with a vengeance and Tom Brady guided his team to a 14-2 record, the best in the league. The Patriots' defense, led by stars like Tedy Bruschi and Richard Seymour, was nearly impenetrable.

In Super Bowl XXXVIII, the Patriots faced the Carolina Panthers in a thrilling contest. Tom Brady's poise under pressure became evident once again as he engineered a game-winning drive in the final minutes. The Patriots secured their second Lombardi Trophy in three years, establishing themselves as a force to be reckoned with.

The following season, the Patriots continued their winning ways. Tom Brady's leadership and precision passing were instrumental in the team's success. The Patriots finished the regular season with a 14-2 record once more, and in Super Bowl XXXIX, they faced the Philadelphia Eagles.

In a hard-fought battle, Tom Brady's ice-cold belief under pressure and sheer determination to win shone once more. He threw for over 230 yards and two touchdowns, leading the Patriots to a 24-21 victory. The back-to-back Super Bowl wins with three Lombardi Trophies in four seasons cemented their status as a modern dynasty. The Patriots achieved the seemingly impossible and Tom Brady's performances in these championship games showcased his ability to deliver in clutch moments, earning him the nickname "Clutch Brady."

As if back-to-back Super Bowls weren't impressive enough, the Patriots aimed for perfection in the 2007 season. Tom Brady, surrounded by a talented roster, orchestrated one of the most prolific offenses in NFL history, throwing for 50 touchdowns and leading the team to an undefeated regular season.

Two playoff wins later, the Patriots marched into Super Bowl XLII with a perfect 18-0 record, poised to make history. However, fate had other plans. In a dramatic clash with the New York Giants, the Patriots fell short, losing 17-14. It was a heartbreaking end to an otherwise spectacular season. Despite the heartbreak of falling short of a perfect season, Tom Brady's individual achievements shone brightly. He set a new NFL record with 50 touchdown passes in a single season, a feat that showcased his unparalleled skill and football IQ.

In the years following 2007, the Patriots remained a perennial contender, thanks in large part to the enduring partnership of Tom Brady and Bill Belichick. They guided the team to another Super Bowl appearance in 2011, where they lost to the Giants once again. "Perhaps the Patriots Era is over," some thought. "Maybe this is as far as Tom Brady can go," others whispered. Those whispers did not last long.

New England returned to the grand stage in 2014 for Super Bowl XLIX against the Seattle Seahawks, and Tom Brady delivered another iconic moment. With the game hanging in the balance, he orchestrated a game-winning drive, culminating in a dramatic touchdown pass to Julian Edelman. The victory solidified the Patriots' status as a modern dynasty, with Tom Brady at the forefront of their success.

Brady became only the third quarterback in NFL history to win the Super Bowl four times and tied Joe Montana's record of three Super Bowl MVP awards.

A game-winning drive is one thing, but in 2016 the Patriots needed a game-winning half as they found themselves 25 points down soon after the midway point of Super Bowl LI against the Atlanta Falcons.

And Tom Brady was about to deliver.

The comeback began with a 75-yard drive that ended in a 5-yard touchdown pass to James White. Stephen Gostkowski hit the upright on the extra point attempt but made amends with a 33-yard field goal after Brady orchestrated another drive of more than 70 yards at the start of the fourth quarter.

It was now 28-12 but there was less than ten minutes left. It was time for the defense to step up. They delivered with a fumble recovery to set up a short drive to the end zone that culminated in a 6-yard touchdown pass to Danny Amendola. White ran in the two-point conversion and suddenly the Patriots were just one score away from tying the game.

The Patriots defense forced the Falcons to punt on their next possession and Brady was handed one last chance. However, there were only three and a half minutes left on the clock and he would have to start from his own nine-yard line.

But this was Tom Brady, and 91-yards later White ran into the end zone again before Brady found Danny Amendola on the two-point conversion attempt to tie the game up.

It was unbelievable, but by now it felt almost inevitable that Brady would cap it all off in overtime. And he did so with an 8-play 75-yard drive to give White a 2-yard run-in and seal one of the most incredible Super Bowl stories ever.

Tom Brady had engineered the greatest comeback in Super Bowl history, once again achieving something that hardly anyone would have thought possible until it happened. And finally, even his biggest critics began to admit that perhaps Brady truly was the greatest of all time. Two years later, Tom and the Patriots won their sixth Super Bowl.

Brady's legacy extended far beyond the trophies. His leadership, work ethic, and ability to elevate his teammates became the standard for excellence in the NFL. The Patriots' dominance became a testament to the enduring brilliance of a quarterback who turned every season into a quest for greatness.

After two decades of unparalleled success with the New England Patriots, Tom Brady shocked the football world by announcing his departure in 2020. The final chapter of his celebrated career would be written with the Tampa Bay Buccaneers.

Brady had always had his doubters and there were many who thought even now that his success was largely down to the brilliant management of Bill Belichick. Here was his chance to show those critics that he truly was the greatest.

Joining forces with an already talented roster, Tom Brady brought his winning mentality to Tampa Bay. In his first season with the Buccaneers, he led them to the Super Bowl LV against the Kansas City Chiefs. At 43 years old, Tom showcased that age was just a number as he secured his seventh Super Bowl victory, further solidifying his legacy as the greatest quarterback of all time.

The journey from a high school bench-rider and overlooked draft pick to the leader of two football powerhouses and seven-time Super Bowl winner is a story of resilience, skill, and an unrelenting pursuit of greatness. The football world had witnessed the making of a living legend – Tom Brady, the quarterback who turned dreams into dynasties.

As Tom Brady approached the twilight of his career, the term "GOAT" (Greatest of All Time) was often used to describe him. But behind the accolades and records, there was a man who never forgot where he came from. He remained close to his family, often sharing the joy of victory and the sting of defeat with them. Off the field, Tom used his success to make a positive impact. He supported various charitable causes and became an inspiration to young athletes everywhere.

In 2022, after 22 incredible seasons in the NFL, the time came for Tom Brady to hang up his cleats and he announced his retirement. The sports world collectively held its breath, realizing that an era had come to an end.

As he walked off the field for the last time, Tom looked back at the remarkable journey that had brought him from a little boy tossing a football in his living room to the greatest quarterback the NFL had ever seen. The cheers of the crowd, the thrill of victory, the lessons learned from setbacks – they were all part of a story that would be told for generations to come: the tale of Tom Brady, the boy who became the GOAT, and entered the annals of sports history. A story of triumph, resilience, and a whole lot of touchdowns.

THE HELMET CATCH

On December 30th, 2007, Tom Coughlin, head coach of the New York Giants came out to meet the press after his team had just lost their final regular season game to New England. The Patriots had come back from 12 points down in the third quarter to win 38-35. Losing always tasted bad but he had to regroup quickly for the postseason, and he knew that preparation for that first wildcard game started here. He gritted his teeth and addressed the reporters in front of him.

"There is nothing but positives", Coughlin insisted. "I told the players in playing this game everything would be positives, there would be no negatives and that is how I feel." In truth there had been little riding on this game for the Giants with their playoff position already secured. Yet this had still been one of the most followed games in NFL history because of what it meant for New England. For the first time since teams had begun playing a 16-game schedule, a franchise had gone the entire regular season undefeated.

"I don't know any better way to be prepared for the playoffs than to go against a team that was 15–0," Coughlin continued. Five weeks later the world would see just how good this preparation had been when the same two teams met in Super Bowl XLII in Glendale, Arizona.

That year, the Patriots had been on a mission – a mission for perfection. They weren't just playing football; they were making history. Tom Brady, the quarterback maestro, was slinging passes like he had a cannon for an arm. The team, led by the genius coach Bill Belichick, was on a winning streak that felt as unstoppable as an avalanche down the side of a mountain.

Game after game, they left a trail of defeated opponents in their wake. Tom Brady was connecting with his receivers like they were sharing secret codes, and the defense was tighter than a jar of pickles.

And they weren't just winning; it was domination. They weren't just beating teams; they were making them question their life choices. The Patriots' offense was like a symphony, and Tom Brady was the conductor, orchestrating touchdowns like they were musical notes.

The Giants' season had gone a little differently. Their star running back Tiki Barber was now retired and their super-talented young quarterback Eli Manning had been struggling to show consistent form. Many were beginning to wonder whether the first overall draft pick would ever live up to expectations.

After losing their first two games of the season, expectations were not high, but the Giants went on to finish the regular season 10-6, secure a wildcard berth in the NFC playoffs and win three postseason games in a row on the road for an unlikely Super Bowl appearance.

The Patriots came into Super Bowl XLII as one of the biggest favorites in NFL history, with the weight of history on their shoulders. But the Giants had shown that they relished the role of underdogs. They were also able to look back on the final game of the regular season and know that they had what it took to go toe-to-toe with this seemingly invincible New England side. They just needed a little more this time round.

The football universe held its breath, wondering if the Patriots could cap off their historic season with the ultimate victory.

The Giants drew first blood after the longest drive in Super Bowl history ended with a field goal after almost ten minutes. The Patriots then scored on their first drive, although it wasn't finished off until the first play of the second quarter, when they were able to run in a touchdown. A defensive battle then ensued, with both teams flexing their muscles and refusing to budge. There would be no more scores for the next half hour of play until the real drama unfolded in the fourth quarter.

Eli Manning, the Giants' quarterback, orchestrated a drive that felt like a symphony of perfect plays. And then, with a flick of his wrist, he connected with David Tyree, a wide receiver who had received few accolades until now, with a 5-yard pass into the end zone for a touchdown. New York now led 10-7.

Then Tom Brady, the quarterback maestro, worked his magic and connected with a wide-open Randy Moss in the end zone for a touchdown. The Patriots retook the lead with under three minutes to go, and it seemed like business as usual. What followed would become the most iconic moment of the game.

Eli Manning had just tried to find Tyree on a second down from his own half and missed due to an apparent miscommunication that left the usually unflappable Manning visibly frustrated. When the ball was snapped for the third down, the New England pass rushers were through the offensive line in a flash and bearing down ominously on the young quarterback. One Patriot missed while two more grabbed fistfuls of Manning's jersey.

Somehow, Eli Manning was able to twist and slip out of their grasps. He reset himself in an instant – that perfect technique that had been honed by a lifetime of preparation kicking in instinctively – and launched the ball downfield. The ball seemed to hang in the air for an age, spiraling its way into Patriot territory.

David Tyree went up for the ball, but so did Pro Bowl safety Rodney Harrison. They both sprang straight up in the air, reaching as far as they possibly could. Tyree should not have had a chance, but somehow when they came down the ball was in Tyree's hands. Or rather it was in one of his hands. Such was the desperation in that play he was unable to clasp it in two hands and had to improvise by pinning the ball to his helmet.

He brilliantly maintained possession all the way to the ground in a move that soon became christened "The Helmet Catch." The pass was complete, and the drive was alive. A few plays later Eli Manning threw a touchdown pass to Plaxico Burress, and the Giants took the lead, 17-14.

The Patriots had one final chance to pull off a miracle though. As the clock ticked down, Tom Brady launched a Hail Mary, but the Giants' defense swatted it away. The final whistle blew, and Super Bowl XLII ended with one of the biggest upsets in NFL history – the New York Giants had beaten the mighty New England Patriots, spoiling their perfect season.

Eli Manning was named the Super Bowl MVP. He stayed calm in the storm, made the right calls, and led his team to victory. It was like a game of chess, and Eli was the grandmaster making all the right moves. But it was David Tyree's catch, which was later dubbed "The Helmet Catch," that became the defining moment when then odds finally swung in New York's favor.

Tyree showed us that sometimes in sports, you need to use your head! In the face of a giant challenge, he didn't back down. He leaped and he stuck his neck out for his team. If he hadn't, he would never have been able to reel in a catch that would be remembered forever. It wasn't just a physical feat; it was a lesson in never giving up, no matter how big the odds.

So, the next time you face a challenge, channel your inner David Tyree. Stick out your helmet, catch that challenge, and show the world that even the little guys can make the biggest plays. Because in the game of life, every catch counts.

THE MANNING FAMILY

Super Bowl XLVI in 2012 took place at Lucas Oil Stadium in Indianapolis and saw the New York Giants face the New England Patriots in a rematch of Super Bowl XLII. As Eli Manning led the New York Giants to their second Super Bowl victory over the Patriots, his older brother Peyton was being interviewed outside the stadium.

Peyton was the star quarterback of the Colts team who called the Lucas Oil Stadium home but had been sidelined by a major neck injury in the 2011 season. It seemed as though the baton of the Manning family football legacy had been passed to Eli and that Peyton's career was destined to be cut short. Many were assuming that Peyton's retirement announcement was just an inevitability. But the man himself had other ideas.

Perhaps the idea of his little brother moving ahead of him in the Super Bowl victories count was too much, but Peyton was determined that his chapter in the Manning family dynasty had a lot more to be written.

As they stood outside the stadium, the interviewer casually asked if he was considering retirement. His response was simple and clear: "I have no plans on doing that."

The Manning family, a name synonymous with pigskin prowess, began its journey towards the stuff of footballing legends with the great Archie Manning. On May 19, 1949, the football gods decided to sprinkle a bit of magic in the town of Drew, Mississippi, and Archie was born to Sis and Buddy Manning.

Growing up in the South, where football is practically a religion, young Archie's childhood was a mix of backyard tosses and Friday night lights. His first love was actually baseball, and many local sporting fans fully expected Archie to find a career in the MLB. But as he grew, so did his love for football. Archie's school days at Drew High were a mix of homework and touchdowns. He became the star quarterback, leading his team to victories that echoed through the small town. The football field became a stage for Archie to showcase his skill and passion.

But life has a way of throwing unexpected passes. In 1969, a somber note struck the Manning tale. Archie lost his father, Buddy Manning, to suicide. It was a tough blow for young Archie, but he would use his father's memory to inspire him. Football would become not just a game but a tribute to his father's memory.

College was the next stop on Archie's wild ride. He packed his bags and headed to the University of Mississippi, or as the folks down there lovingly call it, Ole Miss. College life brought new challenges and triumphs for Archie. The Rebels welcomed him with open arms, and he became a college football sensation. In 1970, he was crowned the Southeastern Conference Player of the Year, a title that solidified his status as a football icon.

Archie's skills on the field couldn't be ignored, and in 1971, he was selected as the second overall pick in the NFL Draft by the New Orleans Saints. The Saints weren't exactly winning Super Bowls left and right, but Archie was the bright spot in the Big Easy.

In 1976, Archie faced a challenge that would test not just his skills on the field but his resilience off it. Knee surgery threatened to sideline him, but Archie, with a determination that would become a Manning trademark, bounced back.

Archie continued to make moves on the field, playing for various teams, including the Houston Oilers and the Minnesota Vikings. He wasn't just a quarterback; he was a symbol of determination and grit. Even when the wins weren't stacking up, Archie kept his head high, showing that true champions aren't defined by scoreboards alone.

In 1985, after 15 seasons in the NFL, he retired from the game he loved. The boy who once tossed a football in his backyard had become a football icon, leaving a legacy that would inspire generations to come. But the story wasn't over for the Manning name in the NFL.

In 1971, Archie had tied the knot with his high school sweetheart, Olivia. Together, they built a family that would become a powerhouse of its own.

Archie Manning, the quarterback extraordinaire embarked on the brand-new adventure of fatherhood in 1974 when his first son, Cooper was born. Now, Cooper may not be as well-known as his younger brothers, but he had a very promising career as a wide receiver ahead of him until he was diagnosed with a condition called spinal stenosis (a narrowing of the spine and pinching of the nerves) whilst playing for Archie's alma mater, Ole Miss.

Then in 1976, the Manning family tree sprouted another quarterback prodigy. Welcome to the world, Peyton Manning! Archie looked down at his newborn son, and maybe, just maybe, he whispered a little something about the magic of football in those tiny ears.

But the Manning football legacy didn't stop there. A few years later, in 1981, Eli Manning, the youngest addition to the Manning quarterback dynasty was born. It was a bit like déjà vu – Archie cradling another tiny bundle of a pigskin prodigy.

As his young boys grew, Archie couldn't resist sharing his passion for football with his little quarterbacks-in-training. But there was no pressure – just a lot of love for the game. Afternoons became family football fiestas as mini footballs flew around the Manning living room. And maybe, just maybe, Archie shared a few of his gridiron secrets with his boys. Perhaps he gathered his little pee wee footballers around to watch some classic footage, narrating the tales of touchdowns past with a twinkle in his eye.

Peyton's high school days at Isidore Newman School were glory days indeed. At this stage he was often throwing touchdown passes to his big brother, Cooper, so Archie must have been doubly proud. By the time he graduated, Peyton had set a gazillion passing records, and college scouts were knocking on his door.

Peyton Manning became the big man on campus at the University of Tennessee and college football had never seen a quarterback quite like him. In 1997, Peyton took home the coveted Maxwell Award and the Davey O'Brien Award, proving he wasn't just a quarterback; he was a gridiron maestro.

The NFL was calling, and Peyton Manning answered. In 1998, the Indianapolis Colts snagged him as the first overall pick in the draft. Peyton wasted no time making his mark, earning NFL Rookie of the Year honors and setting the stage for a career that would be etched in football lore. Peyton Manning, with the arm of a wizard and the mind of a strategist, became the talk of the town.

Eli meanwhile had big shoes to fill, following in the footsteps of his gridiron-legend father and his quarterback-extraordinaire older brother. As a young Manning, Eli's journey into the football realm began much like a sequel to a blockbuster film – the legacy already established, the expectations towering. But Eli Manning wasn't just a shadow; he was a rising star with a determination to craft his own football narrative.

High school days found Eli at Isidore Newman School, where he, too, left an indelible mark on the football field, proving that the Manning magic wasn't a one-brother show.

The spotlight only intensified as he joined the Ole Miss Rebels for his college stint, and like his father before him, Eli became a Southeastern Conference Player of the Year in 2003. The Manning legacy was going from strength to strength.

The NFL beckoned, and in 2004, Eli Manning was selected first overall in the NFL Draft by the San Diego Chargers. But this was just the first chapter in the saga as Eli became part of a trade to the New York Giants.

There were now two Manning brothers playing in the NFL, both extraordinary talents and both ready to write a family legend unlike anything the world of professional football had ever seen.

The 2006 NFL season was when everything came together for Peyton. He led the Colts to a 12-4 regular season record and their fourth AFC South Division title in a row. To Playoff wins against the Chiefs and the Ravens later and they were facing the New England Patriots in the AFC Championship game for a place in Super Bowl XLI.

Peyton threw for almost 350 yards, with one touchdown pass and even a 1-yard touchdown himself, to overturn an 18-point deficit, which was the biggest comeback in a conference championship game in NFL history. AN MVP-winning performance in the Super Bowl against the Chicago Bears and Peyton secured the Manning family's first Lombardi Trophy.

The following season, the family bragging rights would belong to Eli though. With a steely resolve and a dash of Manning magic, he led the New York Giants to victory in Super Bowl XLII. However, this wasn't just a win; it was a David-and-Goliath triumph against the undefeated New England Patriots.

The image of Eli's escape from a seemingly inevitable sack, followed by the iconic "Helmet Catch" by David Tyree, became a defining moment not just for Eli but for the Manning dynasty. In that moment, Eli Manning proved that he wasn't just a quarterback; he was a clutch performer, a maestro under pressure, and a worthy heir to the Manning football legacy.

In 2011, Eli Manning orchestrated another Super Bowl victory, this time against the Patriots again in Super Bowl XLVI. The kid who once threw passes in the shadow of his big brother had become a two-time Super Bowl MVP and a Giants legend. He had also moved to the top rung of the Manning family Super Bowl rings ladder.

His journey hadn't just been a sequel; it was a story of triumph, and a legacy that extended beyond the shadow of his legendary family. Eli Manning, with his own flair and finesse, added a chapter to the Manning football tale that will be retold in football circles for generations to come.

And just as it seemed as though Eli's story was reaching a magical climax, it appeared that Peyton's might be coming to a premature end. In 2011, Peyton Manning found himself facing an opponent more formidable than any linebacker or defensive end.

Leading up to the 2011 season, whispers of discomfort in Peyton's neck grew into a crescendo. Now, this wasn't just any injury; it was a hurdle that threatened to sideline our quarterback extraordinaire for good.

It all came to a head during a routine play at training camp. A seemingly innocent hit, a collision that football players endure regularly, but this time, it had severe consequences. Peyton's neck, the very engine that powered his precise passes and strategic brilliance, bore the brunt of the impact.

The diagnosis was a herniated disc between two of his vertebrae, pressing on nerves and causing an agonizing discomfort that no painkiller could silence. It was a pesky problem that had most likely been brewing over time, silently waiting to throw a wrench into the gears of Manning's illustrious career.

As the pain persisted and the scope of the injury became clearer, Peyton Manning faced a crossroads. It wasn't just about missing a few games – it was about preserving a legacy, about ensuring that the football world wouldn't bid farewell to one of its greatest minds prematurely.

The once unstoppable force of nature was suddenly tethered to the sidelines, watching as his teammates fought battles without their fearless leader. For the first time in a long time, Peyton wasn't orchestrating touchdowns and outsmarting defenses. It was a tough pill to swallow, not just for him but for fans everywhere who had come to expect magic every time he stepped onto the field.

But Peyton Manning wasn't one to back down from a challenge. Instead of throwing in the towel, he rolled up his sleeves and embarked on a journey of recovery that would test not only his physical strength but also his mental fortitude.

His journey through treatment began with a series of surgeries – not just one, but multiple procedures to alleviate the pressure on those crucial nerves.

Physical therapy became a daily ritual, with exercises aimed at rebuilding the strength and flexibility in his neck. Months turned into a grueling year of surgeries, therapies, and doubt. It was a grueling process, but Peyton, with the same determination that made him a football icon, pressed on.

When the 2012 season began, Peyton Manning was set to make his comeback, though he was now a Denver Broncos player after parting ways with the Colts. The anticipation was palpable. Could he recapture the magic that made him a football legend?

Peyton Manning, with a surgically repaired neck and a fire in his belly, played like a man possessed. The football field became his canvas, and every pass was a stroke of brilliance. The Broncos soared to new heights under his command, and once again, Peyton Manning was the talk of the town.

In each of the next three seasons with the Broncos, Peyton would lead them into the playoffs. They even made it all the way to the Super Bowl in his second season with them, but that second Super Bowl victory seemed to elude him.

Again, there was much speculation about whether Peyton's career was over. All acknowledged that he had battled bravely to come back from injury and be as successful as he had been with Denver, and this Denver team had a truly great defense and that enabled them to get off to a 7-0 start. But as the 2015 season progressed, he seemed to be struggling for form. In week 10 he surpassed Brett Favre's record for career passing yards but was later benched with an injury that kept him out the following week.

Brock Osweiler filled in and did such a good job that when Manning returned for the final game of the regular season, he was only the backup quarterback – something he had not experienced since his freshman year at college. However, this was the end of Osweiler's run of form and he was benched in favor of Manning after throwing two interceptions and fumbling once. Manning was able to lead the Broncos to victory and remained at the helm for their playoff run that culminated in his fourth Super Bowl appearance.

Super Bowl 50 was to be the toughest test of Denver's incredible defense as they came up against the league-leading offense of the Carolina Panthers, spearheaded by the flamboyant season MVP Cam Newton – a quarterback who was thirteen years younger than Peyton Manning. Denver's defense won the day, but Manning also had his say. His final pass of the game was a touchdown reception by Bennie Fowler that sealed a 24-10 win for the Broncos. This was to be the final pass of Peyton Manning's career.

It was a gritty win that perfectly reflected Mannings intelligence, fortitude and determination. In Peyton's own words, "It's not wanting to win that makes you a winner; it's refusing to fail."

In a game that showcased his strategic brilliance and unrivaled determination, Peyton Manning led the Broncos to victory. The final whistle blew, confetti rained down, and Peyton stood tall, not just as a two-time Super Bowl champion but as a living testament to the power of perseverance.

The Manning family continue to hold a special place in the hearts of all football fans and regularly appear on TV offering their brilliant insights into the nuances of this wonderful sport. And with Cooper Manning's son, Arch, showing promise as a college quarterback with the Texas Longhorns, perhaps we've not yet seen the end of the on-field Manning magic either.

The Manning saga might yet have another chapter waiting to unfold, but they have already made a greater impact on the NFL than any other football family. With Archie's gridiron glory, Peyton's comeback magic and Eli's Super Bowl heroics, the Mannings became a football dynasty for the ages. Together they have woven a tapestry of triumph, resilience, and the true spirit of the game.

JERRY "FLASH 80" RICE

A brutal tussle of a football game was taking place under the bright lights of Joe Robbie Stadium in Miami, Florida on January 22, 1989. The San Francisco 49ers were facing the Cincinnati Bengals in Super Bowl XXIII and for almost three quarters of the game, defenses had been on top. San Francisco had just tied the game up again at 6-6 in the third quarter. But then something happened that threatened to shatter the dreams of every 49ers player and fan watching.

From the ensuing kickoff, the Bengals returned the ball all the way into the end zone in a stunning special teams play that handed Cincinnati a seven-point lead. In the context of such a tight game, this could be a game-winning score.

Jerry Rice got to his feet on the San Francisco sideline and looked around him. After four seasons in the league, he had established himself as the premier wide receiver in the NFL through talent, skill and a whole lot of hard work. But he was desperate for the Super Bowl ring to cap that all off.

His team had their backs up against the wall. It was time for the offense to step up and take hold of this game. And Jerry Rice was never one to shy away from a challenge.

With the quiet determination and steely resolve that characterized everything this great man did, he donned his helmet and ran out onto the field to get to work. The 49ers huddled up and star quarterback, Joe Montana called a short pass to Jerry Rice. The players broke from their huddle and lined up to start their make-or-break drive.

Like a footballing machine Jerry Rice visualized the play to come in his head as he waited for the snap, mapping his route across the field as if looking at the game from above. He knew exactly where he was going to break and exactly where he needed to be to catch Montana's pass.

He glanced at the cornerback lining up to mark him. Frankly, it wouldn't have mattered if there were three of them or none at all. This was his moment.

The center snapped the ball, and Jerry Rice was gone.

Jerry Lee Rice was born on October 13, 1962 in the sunny town of Starkville, Mississippi. Jerry's childhood was happy but not the easiest. His dad, Joe Nathan Rice, was a brick mason, and his mom, Eddie B. Rice, worked hard cleaning the houses of wealthier families.

They didn't have much, but they had each other. From a young age Jerry and his siblings would have to work to help their parents make ends meet.

Sometimes they would go to building sites with their dad and carry bricks to make sure that he always had a ready supply to hand. On occasions this would involve one of them throwing bricks up to the other who was further up the scaffolding where their dad was working. Perhaps this was how Jerry developed his unearthly catching ability. Other times they would work on local farms picking corn, cotton, hay, or whatever they needed to do to help their parents put food on the table. Jerry always said that all this taught him the meaning of hard work. This incredible work ethic was a characteristic that would go on to help make him the greatest wide receiver of all time.

Jerry was a shy child and, though fit and active, still hadn't really shown his sporting talent by the time he started high school. Then one day he was caught skipping a class by the school principal and ran for it. No doubt he got in a bit of trouble – not least from his parents – but the overriding impression from the teacher was, "Wow, that kid is fast!"

The principal made sure to inform the coach of the football team of Jerry's speed and he was asked to try out for the squad. Eddie B was reluctant to let her precious son get involved in such a violent sport, but the candle had been lit. Jerry wanted this, and as soon as his mother realized the talent he had, and how alive sport had made her son, that was it.

He joined the B.L. Moor High School football team, where he honed his skills and showcased his incredible speed and agility. The football field became Jerry's second home, and he spent countless hours practicing his moves, perfecting his catches, and sprinting down the field like a gazelle. He tried multiple positions, including running back and tight end. But it soon became clear that he was a naturally gifted wide receiver.

He continued to use the things that made his childhood hard to his advantage as he took his training more seriously. He would run the several-mile trip back home after school each day because he didn't have a ride, and he became supremely fit. By the time he was a junior, he was a high school football legend, wowing his tiny community with skills the likes of which they had never seen.

As the years passed, Jerry's talent on the football field couldn't be ignored. College scouts from prestigious universities took notice of the young star, and Jerry found himself with a golden opportunity. He accepted a scholarship to play football at Mississippi Valley State University, largely because of the reputation the school had for its emphasis on passing. Their gunslinging offense was the perfect foil for Jerry's skills.

Rice shone alongside his friend and teammate quarterback Willie Totten and together they became known as the 'Starlight Express.' Mississippi Valley State had an offense that was wildly adventurous, often lining four receivers up on the same side of the field. Jerry was flourishing, but life was still tough. Balancing academics and athletics was no easy feat, and Jerry often had to rely on his friends for food because his scholarship didn't allow him enough to satisfy the appetite of such a fierce athlete.

Jerry's record-setting college career earned him the nickname, 'World' for his incredible catching ability. His college years culminated in an MVP performance in the College All-Star game, the Blue-Gray Classic in 1984 and an NCAA record for total career touchdown receptions. The next chapter of his life was about to unfold. In 1985, the NFL Draft rolled around, and Jerry was on the brink of realizing a dream he had held since childhood. The San Francisco 49ers selected him as the 16th overall pick, marking the beginning of a stellar professional career.

Joining the 49ers was a dream come true for Jerry, but the transition to the NFL wasn't without its share of obstacles. The competition was fierce, and the speed of the game was on a whole new level. Yet, Jerry faced these challenges with the same determination and tenacity that had propelled him through high school and college. And just as had been the case through high school and college, the thing that truly made him exceptional was that unparalleled work ethic.

"Today I will do what others won't," he would say to himself, "so that tomorrow I can do what others can't." This was the gritty, professional attitude that would characterize Jerry Rice's entire career.

In his rookie season, Jerry quickly adapted to the professional stage, showcasing his exceptional skills. His precise route-running and reliable hands made him a favorite target for the 49ers' quarterbacks. As the team soared to new heights, Jerry's star continued to rise.

In the 49ers final game of the regular season, Rice had seven receptions for 111 yards and even scored a rushing touchdown. It was a performance that prompted one television announcer to declare that, "When this guy is finished, he'll be considered one of the greatest wide receivers to ever play this game."

Despite only starting four regular season games and one playoff, Jerry finished the season with over fifty receptions for nearly a thousand yards. For most NFL rookies, this sort of first season as a pro would have been a stellar achievement. For Jerry Rice it was just the first step. His first year had shown him what playing in the NFL was really like and what he needed to do to elevate his performances to the next level.

He spent his first off season studying the 49ers playbook until he not only knew it by heart, but he understood the intricacies of every moving piece.

His reputation continued to grow over the following seasons, and he continued to push himself to new heights. Then everything seemed to come together for the 49ers in the 1988 season as they marched towards the Lombardi Trophy and the greatest prize in the game.

Super Bowl XXIII took place at Joe Robbie Stadium in Miami, Florida. The 49ers faced off against the Cincinnati Bengals in a closely contested match. The tension in the air was palpable as the 49ers aimed for their third Super Bowl victory. Little did the fans know that they were about to witness a masterclass performance by Jerry Rice.

The first half was tense, with both teams testing the waters and defenses dominating. The 49ers struck first with a first quarter field goal from Mike Cofer. The Bengals responded with a field goal of their own in the second quarter, courtesy of Jim Breech and the game was tied at 3-3 at half time.

In the second half, the Bengals went on a grinding 61-yard drive that took nearly ten minutes. But at the end of all that, the 49ers held them to a field goal. With less than a minute left in the quarter, the 49ers were trailing 3-6 before Mike Cofer tied things up with a 32-yard field goal.

Cofer's next kick on the very next play would end in disaster though, as Stanford Jennings returned the San Francisco kickoff 93 yards for the first touchdown of the game. This gritty wrestling match of a football game had suddenly been blown wide open as the Bengals took the biggest lead of the night and went up 13-6.

With just over a quarter remaining in the game, the 49ers were up against it and needed their stars to come out and shine. They needed a big drive to turn the game around... and they got it.

It began with a pass to Jerry Rice and the star receiver managed to turn Joe Montana's short throw into a 31-yard gain. The 49ers were off and running. Then came a pivotal moment in Jerry's career.

With lightning speed and precision, he eluded defenders and sprinted down the field on the fourth play of the drive. Joe Montana dropped back to pass. He looked downfield, scanning the field for an open receiver. And then he saw him. Jerry Rice, streaking down the field.

Montana threw the ball, a perfect spiral that sailed through the air. Rice ran faster, his legs pumping like pistons. He leaped into the air, his arms outstretched. The ball hit his hands, and he reeled it in, pulling it in close to his body. He landed on the ground, his feet still moving, his eyes fixed on the end zone. The crowd erupted in cheers as Rice danced in and lifted the ball held high above his head in celebration.

With less than a quarter of the game remaining, they were tied at 13-13. The 49ers were back in business, but this game still had a long way to go.

The 49ers forced a punt on the Bengals' next possession but then missed a field goal that would have given them the lead. That error was compounded when Cincinnati scored the go ahead field goal on their next drive. They were 16-13 up.

The clock ticked down, and with just over three minutes remaining, the stage was set for a legendary drive. In a moment that would be forever etched in football history, Joe Montana orchestrated a masterful 92-yard drive, most of that yardage coming in three completions to the ever-reliable Jerry Rice, who was now on his way to a 200-yard performance on the night.

The drive reached a climax with 39 seconds left in the game, when Joe Montana dropped back to pass and saw John Taylor, streaking towards the end zone. Montana threw the ball, another perfect spiral that found Taylor for a 10-yard game-winning touchdown.

The stadium erupted in cheers as Jerry Rice and everyone else who had anything to do with the 49ers organization, raised their arms in triumph and celebrated the score that would secure the San Francisco victory. The final score: 49ers 20, Bengals 16.

Super Bowl XXIII had delivered a spectacle for the ages, and Jerry Rice's contribution had been nothing short of extraordinary, catching 11 passes for 215 yards and a touchdown. His jaw-dropping catches and ground-breaking performance earned him the Super Bowl MVP award. He had reached the very top, but he wanted to stay there a little longer.

The 49ers defended the Super Bowl title in convincing fashion the following year with a 55-10 victory over the Denver Broncos. Then, as the '80s gave way to the '90s, Jerry's career continued to soar to unprecedented heights. With the retirement of Joe Montana, San Francisco soon found themselves another legendary quarterback in Steve Young. And just like his predecessor, Young formed a superhuman partnership with Jerry Rice.

In 1995, and the San Francisco 49ers were once again on the grand stage of the Super Bowl, this time facing the San Diego Chargers in Super Bowl XXIX. The stage was set for another epic clash, and at the heart of the action was none other than the legendary Jerry Rice, poised to create more football history.

The game took place at Joe Robbie Stadium in Miami, Florida, creating a sense of déjà vu for the 49ers and their fans, and right from the kickoff, it was clear that the 49ers were going to be a force to be reckoned with.

The first quarter saw quarterback Steve Young connecting with Jerry Rice for an early 44-yard passing touchdown, which set the tone for a high-scoring affair. Rice would reel in two more touchdown receptions that night as the 49ers streaked to victory by a margin of 49-26.

The streets of San Francisco erupted in celebration, and Jerry's infectious grin mirrored the joy of the entire city. His ability to rise to the occasion on the biggest stage further solidified his status, and he had once again proven that when it came to football excellence, he was in a league of his own. Jerry Rice had also become the defining icon in a glorious period in the history of the San Francisco 49ers, bridging the tenure of two legendary quarterbacks and confirming his position as the finest wide receiver to ever play the game.

In 1997, he was traded to the Oakland Raiders. The change was bittersweet, as Jerry left behind the team and fans that had become like family. However, true to his resilient nature, Jerry embraced the new chapter in his career with characteristic determination, and the move proved to be a wise decision for Jerry. In 2002, he experienced another career highlight when the Raiders reached Super Bowl XXXVII. Although they fell short of victory, Jerry's performance on the grand stage demonstrated that he was still a force to be reckoned with, even in the later years of his career.

Jerry's career was a testament to the power of hard work, resilience, and a positive attitude. In 2004, at the age of 42, He officially retired from professional football. The news sent shockwaves through the sports world, marking the end of an era. Jerry Rice had left an indelible mark on the NFL, and his legacy would continue to inspire aspiring athletes for generations to come. Despite his success, Jerry remained humble and grounded and he credited his upbringing and the unwavering support of his family for his achievements.

Jerry Rice's lasting legacy in the world of football is nothing short of legendary. His career is adorned with an array of records that stand as a testament to his unparalleled skill and longevity in the NFL. When he retired, he had accrued 13 Pro Bowl selections and three Super Bowl rings, as well as holding records for the most career receptions (1,549), the most career receiving yards (22,895), the most career touchdown receptions (197), the most receptions in a single season (122 in 1995) and the most receiving yards in a single season (1,848 in 1995 again), as well as many, many more.

It was fair to say that Jerry Rice held just about all of the major NFL receiving records, not only showcasing his individual brilliance but also highlighting his remarkable consistency and durability over the course of his illustrious career.

But his legacy extends beyond the numbers. His work ethic, discipline, and love for the game have left an indelible mark on the sport. Known for his precise route-running, sure hands, and ability to perform in clutch moments, Rice set a standard for excellence that aspiring wide receivers still look up to and will do for decades to come.

The story of Jerry Rice, the small-town boy with a big dream, continues to echo through the annals of sports history. His legacy lives on in the hearts of fans, the records he set, and the lessons he taught. Jerry Rice will forever be remembered not just as a football legend but as an embodiment of the spirit of determination, resilience, and the joy of the game.

He is held in the very highest regard by his peers, coaches, and fans alike. His name is synonymous with greatness, and his influence reaches far beyond the football community. The respect he garnered throughout his career is a testament to his sportsmanship, leadership, and unwavering commitment to excellence.

In the grand narrative of NFL history, Jerry Rice's chapter stands out as a shining example of what can be achieved through talent, hard work, and passion. As the years pass, Jerry Rice's name remains etched in the record books, a symbol of football excellence that will continue to inspire and resonate with fans for generations to come. His legacy is not just a part of NFL history; it is a timeless story of greatness that transcends the boundaries of the sport.

"THE CATCH"

The air was thick with anticipation as the clock ticked down on a chilly January day in 1982 for the climax of that season's NFC Championship game. The San Francisco 49ers and the Dallas Cowboys were locked in a duel that would be remembered for ages.

San Francisco needed a last gasp touchdown. They were 89 yards from the end zone with less than five minutes on the clock. But they had Joe Montana, and so they always had a chance.

Over the course of the next thirteen plays, Montana demonstrated why he was one of the very best the game had ever seen, as he managed a perfectly organized drive that took the 49ers to within six yards of glory.

As the 49ers huddled up, Joe Montana, the quarterback with nerves of steel, surveyed the field. The Cowboys' defense, determined to thwart any attempt, resembled a wall of knights guarding a castle. Montana knew he needed something magical, something extraordinary.

With the score tight and tension high, it was time for the defining moment – the play that would go down in history as "The Catch."

This was a crossroads in NFL history. The Cowboys had been the dominant force for a decade but here were a bunch of pretenders to the throne dressed in red and gold and led by a truly gifted quarterback in Joe Montana. The 49ers were on a quest for glory. The Cowboys stood in their way like formidable dragons guarding a treasure. Would the Cowboys dynasty continue or would this game mark the rising of a new star in the football universe.

The Cowboys, with their star-studded roster, had been a force to be reckoned with throughout the season. Led by the seasoned quarterback, Danny White, they carved a path through their opponents like a band of noble heroes on a quest. Each victory added a jewel to their crown, and the Cowboys were determined to add the ultimate gem – the Super Bowl title. Throughout the season, the Cowboys showcased their prowess on the field. From thrilling victories against fierce rivals to dramatic comebacks that left fans on the edge of their seats, they demonstrated the heart of true champions.

On the other side of the NFC football kingdom, the 49ers were crafting their own tale of triumph. Joe Montana, the quarterback with a golden arm, led his team with a mix of skill and charisma.

The 49ers, like a group of underdog heroes, had faced challenges and doubters, but they persevered, winning crucial battles that paved their way to the championship game.

And now these two titans of the National Football Conference clashed with a place in the Super Bowl at stake. By the end of this game, one team would edge a step closer to the big prize, while the other would be back to square one and have to begin the tortuous off-season months of waiting for their next shot at glory.

The atmosphere was electric as the teams took the field. The fans roared like a stampede of wild animals, and you could feel the excitement in the air. The 49ers were determined. The Cowboys were resolute. The game was epic.

The kickoff was like the sounding of a trumpet, signaling the beginning of a fierce battle. The 49ers defense forced the Cowboys to punt off their first possession and then their offense got to work. Montana orchestrated a masterful drive down the field. It was like watching a wizard cast a spell with his magical arm and he finished the drive off with an 8-yard touchdown pass to wide receiver Freddie Solomon. The 49ers defense again frustrated the Cowboys but this time they did at least manage to get into field goal range and kicker Rafael Septien got them on the board.

It was all going to plan for the 49ers. They were 7-3 up and had possession of the football. But then running back Bill Ring fumbled and handed the ball back to Dallas in excellent field position. White seized the chance and put the Cowboys ahead with a 26-yard touchdown pass to Tony Hill.

As the game unfolded, it became a rollercoaster of emotions. One moment, the 49ers soared like eagles, and the next, the Cowboys fought back like determined warriors. The back-and-forth struggle had the crowd gasping in amazement and clutching their lucky charms.

Another touchdown each had the Cowboys up 17-14 at halftime. Many football fans could feel the ominous inevitability of another Dallas victory and yet another Super Bowl appearance looming on the horizon. But these 49ers were not finished yet.

In the face of adversity, Montana rallied his troops. He spoke words of encouragement that echoed through the locker room like a motivational speech from a wise old sage.

The team listened with determination in their faces, ready to face whatever challenges lay ahead.

The two teams retook the field for the second half and exchanged interceptions in the third quarter before a 2-yard touchdown run from running back Johnny Davis put San Francisco back in front 21-17. But by the first minute of the fourth quarter a Dallas field goal cut the lead to just a single point.

Things got even darker for Niners fans when running back Walt Easley fumbled to hand the ball back to Dallas at midfield. White was soon throwing a 21-yard touchdown pass to tight end Doug Cosbie to give the Cowboys a 27-21 lead. An interception on San Francisco's next possession put the Cowboys on the brink of yet another shot at the Lombardi Trophy.

But the 49ers defense stepped up and forced the Cowboys to punt. Joe Montana would have one last chance to drive his team down the field. They needed a touchdown and he had to start from his own 11-yard line, but Montana orchestrated the drive perfectly and four minutes later the 49ers found themselves just six yards from the promised land of the end zone.

The ball was snapped, and like a wizard conjuring a spell, Montana dropped back, scanning the field with the precision of a hawk eyeing its prey. The Cowboys' defense, relentless in their pursuit, closed in, creating a maelstrom of chaos. It was a moment that felt like an eternity, a heartbeat suspended in time.

And then, in a burst of brilliance, Montana decided to go to his backup target – Dwight Clark. The wide receiver, with a heart pounding in rhythm with the crowd, had sprinted to the back of the end zone and cut sideways, creating separation from his defender and just staying in bounds.

The Cowboys' defenders created a wall in front of Montana so that he couldn't actually see his target, but he knew exactly where Clark would be. He fired and the ball soared through the air, like an enchanted orb guided by fate itself.

Clark, with a grace that seemed almost otherworldly, leaped into the air impossibly high. It was as if time slowed down, and for a brief moment, he hung in mid-air like a celestial being defying gravity. His outstretched hands reached for the ball, and at that very instant, a hush fell over the stadium.

The defense was so intense that Montana had been forced into throwing the ball so high that even with his receiver at full stretch and jumping impossibly high, Clark could still only get fingertips to the ball. But fingertips were enough.

The crowd watched with bated breath as Clark pulled the ball securely into his grasp.

Joe Montana had been knocked to the ground by the blitzing defenders after releasing the ball, and all he could see from his vantage point on the grass was Clark's feet touching down after his leap. But the explosion of elated screams from the crowd told him that the catch was good.

The stadium erupted in a cacophony of roars, as if the very earth had joined in the celebration. The 49ers' faithful, witnessing this magical spectacle, felt a surge of joy that could only be described as euphoric. The cheers were deafening as the 49ers secured their victory. The heroes had triumphed, and the fans rejoiced as if they had just witnessed a miracle.

"The Catch," as the play became known, symbolized the culmination of a season filled with trials and tribulations. Montana and Clark, in their mystical connection, had forged a moment that would echo through the halls of football history.

In the Super Bowl that followed two weeks later, the 49ers would finish the job. They got off to a great start, scoring 20 points in the first half. The Bengals fought back in the second half, but the 49ers' lead proved to be too much. The 49ers won the game 26-21, earning their first Super Bowl victory. Joe Montana turned in an MVP performance in that game, throwing for 157 yards, one touchdown, and also running in a touchdown himself.

But it was the result in the NFC championship game that would later be heralded as a turning point in the balance of power in the NFC, with the Cowboys' decade of dominance coming to an end and the beginning of what would be a golden era for the 49ers and indeed for the whole NFL.

THE BIRTH OF THE ICONIC HUDDLE

The year was 1894, on a crisp October afternoon on the campus of Gallaudet University in Washington, D.C. The leaves painted the campus in shades of orange and red, and the faint smell of autumn lingered in the air. Gallaudet, a college for the deaf, was preparing to face another deaf team, a contest marked by both anticipation and rivalry.

But this time, as the Gallaudet players congregated on the field, something unusual happened. Instead of the customary pre-game milling about, they came together shoulder to shoulder, forming an unusually tight circle. Heads inclined towards each other, their formation was a scene of deliberate unity, a curious sphere of concentration.

Amidst the loud cheers and sounds of the stadium, some onlookers gazed at them in confusion, wondering what this unconventional assembly signified. Little did they know, this was the birth of an ingenious strategy that would leave an unforgettable mark on the game of football

Rewind to earlier that season. Paul Hubbard, the quarterback for Gallaudet's football team, faced a unique challenge. His team used sign language to communicate, an advantage against hearing teams but a vulnerability against other deaf teams who could see and understand their signs. Paul knew he needed a strategy to conceal their plays. As he pondered this dilemma, his eyes fell upon his teammates, standing in a close-knit group. His teammates' natural inclination to cluster together, sparking a ground-breaking idea. In a pivotal game, the Gallaudet players, upon Hubbard's discrete cue, came together in a close-knit huddle, turning their backs to their opponents. Within this shielded circle, their hands flew in swift, silent conversation, articulating strategies invisible to the rival team. This ingenious formation, the huddle, became their secret weapon, cloaking their tactics in mystery. The opposing team watched, puzzled and unable to decipher the signs hidden within this protective cocoon. The "huddle," as it would come to be known, was a simple yet brilliant solution, born out of necessity and ingenuity.

The Gallaudet team used this technique to great effect, surprising their opponents with plays that seemed to materialize out of thin air. Their success caught the attention of other teams, and soon, the huddle became a standard practice in football, used by deaf and hearing teams alike. It was a strategic innovation, a way to communicate and unite the team in a single, focused moment.

Today, the huddle is a staple of football, a symbol of teamwork and strategy. But its origins are often overlooked, rooted in the silent world of sign language and the ingenuity of a deaf quarterback. Paul Hubbard didn't just create a tactic; he brought a new dimension to the game, a testament to the power of adaptation and the universal language of sport.

So, every time you see a football team gather in a huddle, remember its origins on a small college field in D.C., where a group of deaf players and their innovative quarterback reshaped the game in a way that speaks volumes, even in silence.

THE "HAIL MARY" MIRACLE

It was December 28, 1975, in Metropolitan Stadium, Bloomington, Minnesota, a setting where winter's chill wrapped itself around every spectator. The crowd huddled together for warmth, their breath misting in the air.

The late afternoon sky, a canvas of dusky hues, served as the backdrop for a moment soon to be etched in football lore.

The tension was high as the game neared its climax.

This was not just any play; it was one of the final acts of a fiercely contested battle, a do-or-die moment with mere seconds left on the clock.

The Cowboys, trailing and with their backs against the wall, were on the brink of playoff elimination.

The crowd held its breath. The seconds on the clock were ticking away... 3... 2... 1... Roger Staubach, the young Navy quarterback, whipped his arm forward, sending the football spiraling into the air, a desperate arc across the dusky sky.

Just as he released the ball, he closed his eyes briefly and muttered the sheepish and hopeful word "Hail Mary.", under his breath. The ball, like a comet against the twilight, found its way into the arms of wide receiver Terry Orr.

Touchdown!

In the post-game interview, when asked about that final play, Roger simply said, "I closed my eyes and said a Hail Mary." This off-the-cuff remark not only described his mindset during the play but also unknowingly coined a term that would become synonymous with long, desperate passes in football and beyond.

The term "Hail Mary" was, for Roger, not just a football reference but also a reflection of his deep-rooted faith. He was known to be a devout Catholic, and in that moment of desperation, he instinctively turned to his faith for a glimmer of hope. It was a nod to the Hail Mary prayer, a powerful Catholic invocation seeking the intercession of the Virgin Mary, asking for her guidance and blessings.

This miraculous throw, forever known in football history as the "Hail Mary," transcended the realm of sports. Over time, the term "Hail Mary" has permeated various domains, becoming a universal metaphor for any last-ditch effort made against seemingly insurmountable odds. It's a phrase that encapsulates hope, a prayer for success when the odds are stacked against you.

So, when you hear someone refer to a "Hail Mary" in sports, business, or everyday life, remember the cold December day in 1975, when Roger Staubach's throw against the twilight sky wrote a new chapter in the lexicon of American culture.

THE FIRST FOOTBALL GAME EVER

It's November 6, 1869, in New Brunswick, New Jersey. The chilly autumn air and the excited chatter of students and locals alike fills the air, as they gather around a field at Rutgers University. They're about to witness a historic clash — the very first football game. Ever. The teams? Rutgers vs Princeton. But, unlike the football we know today, this game had its roots in soccer, with a round ball and rules adapted from the London Football Association. Unlike the padded warriors of modern football, these young athletes are dressed in simple, everyday attire — no helmets, no shoulder pads, just their college clothes, perhaps a little sturdier for the game. It's a far cry from today's protective gear.

With the unusually high number of 25 players on each side, these pioneering athletes were ready to play. But here is the kicker - No one can carry or throw the ball — only kicking is allowed. The goal? To score by getting the ball into the opponent's territory.

The game consisted of 10 rounds, each ending when a goal was scored. The team with the most goals after these rounds would emerge victorious.

Rutgers scored first, with a strategic "flying wedge" play, a formation allowing them to charge at the defenders. Princeton soon adapted, and "Big Mike" Michael, a notable player, disrupted Rutgers' formation to even the score. A key player for Rutgers was Madison M. Ball, a Civil War veteran, whose quick reflexes and unique heel-kick technique kept Princeton at bay and helped Rutgers regain the lead.

The match was intense, marked by headlong running, wild shouting, and frantic kicking. The strategy was simple yet physically demanding. Despite Princeton's size advantage, their struggle with team kicking allowed the more agile Rutgers players to outmaneuver them. This agility, coupled with Rutgers captain John W. Leggett's tactic to keep the ball low, thwarted Princeton's taller players, leading to Rutgers' historic 6-4 victory.

But wait, our story doesn't end there. Enter Walter Camp, a Yale man, who would transform this rugby-like game into the football we adore today. Camp, a Yale undergraduate and medical student from 1876 to 1881, playing halfback at the time, was a visionary on the football field. After countless hours on the field he saw facets of the game that could be optimized. He didn't just play the game; he reimagined it.

He was the mastermind who proposed replacing the chaotic scrummage with the orderly line of scrimmage. He introduced the system of downs, the snap-back from the center, and the formation of an 11-man team.

This Yale legend even created the quarterback position and the scoring scale we use in football today. Imagine the game evolving, play by play, rule by rule, under Camp's guidance.

But the story of football is not just about rules and gameplay. It's about the spirit, the strategy, and the heart-pounding excitement that fills a stadium. Walter Camp, known as the "Father of American Football," was not just a player or a coach; he was a revolutionary who saw the potential of a game and transformed it into a sport that would become a cornerstone of American culture.

So, next time you watch a football game, remember this tale. Remember the crisp November day in New Jersey when Rutgers and Princeton kicked off the journey. Remember Walter Camp, who shaped the chaos into strategy and gave us the thrilling game of American football we cherish today.

CONCLUSION

Whew! What an extraordinary journey it's been, huh? We've soared alongside legends like Tom "The Bomb" Dempsey, marvelled at the unstoppable force of Tom Brady, and revelled in the blazing speed of Jerry "Flash 80" Rice. We've also witnessed the awe-inspiring unbeaten season of the Miami Dolphins and the birth of the iconic huddle that changed the game.

These stories, whether about legendary athletes or unforgettable moments, remind us that football is not just a game; it's a tapestry of courage, determination, and the unshakable belief that anything is possible. These heroes and moments have shaped the sport we love, and their stories will stay with us, inspiring us to reach for the stars and chase our own dreams.

As you close this book and place it on your shelf, remember that you now carry a piece of football history with you. Let these stories be your playbook for life, guiding you in moments of triumph and helping you stand strong in the face of adversity.

Thanks for joining us on this incredible journey through the world of football. Keep cheering, keep dreaming, and most importantly, keep being the extraordinary, unique YOU.

Remember, these stories aren't just tales of greatness; they're a reminder that your own story of greatness is just beginning!

Made in United States
Troutdale, OR
04/02/2024

18882233R00046